THE EARTH SPIRIT

SPIRIT

Its Ways, Shrines and Mysteries

JOHN MICHELL

With 113 illustrations, 22 in color

THAMES AND HUDSON

ART AND IMAGINATION
General Editor: Jill Purce

Published in the United States of America in 1989 by
Thames and Hudson Inc., 500 Fifth Avenue,
New York, New York 10110
Reprinted 1992

Library of Congress Catalog Card Number 88-50255

Printed and bound in Singapore

The Earth Spirit:
its Ways, Shrines and Mysteries

The first men, by all traditional accounts, lived in perfect harmony with nature and the gods. Of their own accord, said Ovid, without the compulsion of law, they were honest and true. There was no punishment or fear, no judges or soldiers. 'The earth itself gave all things spontaneously, and men were content with its uncultivated produce.' Plato in his *Laws* refers to Hesiod's myth of the age of Cronus, when 'all that life requires was provided unasked and in abundance', the reason being that the men of that time were ruled not by other men but by spirits, these corresponding to the eternal element in human nature. The men of the age of Cronus were wanderers, living under the direct guidance and protection of the earth spirit, following the migratory paths of their ancestors, vitally concerned with the cycles of animal and plant life, the progress of the seasons, the movements of the heavenly bodies. Perambulating each year the wide range of their native territory, they traced the steps of the gods who first created it, thus living out a cosmogony in which every spot, every feature of the landscape had its mythical significance, reflected in the activities that took place there. Time was cyclical, not linear; creation was a continuous process, and the spirits that promoted it were ubiquitous and eternal.

From each station on the year's journey the sun and moon were seen rising and setting at certain positions on the horizon, and the same configurations of the stars were observed, constant for many lifetimes and only varying, like the people's habits, in the course of astronomical ages. So it was that every place became associated with a

day of the year and a plan of the heavenly bodies. On that day, marked by the rise of a familiar star, the local deities were active, speaking to the people in their dreams and intuitions and providing fruits of the earth appropriate to the season. This was the style of the golden age, when men lived in the paradisial garden for which they were designed, as intimate with the vital spirit of the earth as was Adam with his Creator, yet no more concerned with religion, spirituality and formal ritual than they were with science, philosophy, usury or political economy. The earth was sacred, not because pious people chose so to regard it, but because it was in fact ruled by spirit, by the creative powers of the universe, manifest in all the phenomena of nature, shaping the features of the landscape, regulating the seasons, the cycles of fertility, the lives of animals and men. In this secure, immortal world the most assured reality was communication with the local gods, personifying aspects of the universal spirit of the earth. Rocks, trees, mountains, wells and springs were recognized as receptacles for spirit, displaying in season their various properties, fertilizing, therapeutic and oracular. The ancients, as Socrates remarked, had no pretensions to cleverness and were quite prepared to listen to a rock or oak tree if only it spoke the truth.

Before civilization sets in, the earth is the one universal deity; not the material earth, but the spirit by virtue of which, according to the ancient philosophers, it is a living creature: a female, because it receives the power of the sun, is animated thereby and made fertile. The body of the earth, like the body of a man, is corruptible and subject to change, but its spirit is unchanging, and therefore the essential nature of this planetary being is spiritual; indeed, Porphyry states that the physical earth is merely a symbol of the earth as it really is. The orthodox view that survived into the middle ages from prehistoric times is expressed by the alchemist Basilius Valentinus: 'The earth is not a dead body, but is inhabited by a spirit that is its life and soul. All created things, minerals included, draw their strength from the earth spirit. This spirit is life, it is nourished by the stars, and it gives nourishment to all the living things it shelters in its womb. Through the spirit received from on high, the earth hatches the minerals in her womb as the mother her unborn child.' Man in his natural state, enjoying the abundance of the virgin earth, considers any proposal to violate it, or to modify in any way its superficial appearance, to be sacrilegious as well as superfluous; in token of which is the dignified protest by the American Indian prophet, Smohalla, against the proposal to turn his people into cultivators:

'My young men shall never work. Men who work can not dream, and wisdom comes to us in dreams. You ask me to plough the ground. Shall I take a knife and tear my mother's breast? Then when I die she will not take me to her bosom to rest. You ask me to dig for stone. Shall I dig under her skin for her bones? Then when I die I can not enter her body to be born again. You ask me to cut grass and make hay and sell it and be rich like white men. But how dare I cut off my mother's hair?'

This most orthodox sentiment is a universal theme of prophecy.

The oldest and deepest element in any religion is the cult of the earth spirit in her many aspects. Especially to wandering men, nomads, pilgrims, itinerants, tramps and half-wits, she is the mother, and they, her children, partake of her sanctity. The pious duty of settled people is hospitality to travellers, for they are acolytes of Hermes, the errant spirit of earth, who, as Mercurius, is also the Virgin; and even now the cult that Protestants unkindly call Mariolatry flourishes spontaneously within the Roman Catholic Church and would do so independently were it not recognized by the hierarchy. In Ireland and other Catholic countries, feasts such as the Assumption of the Virgin on August 15th are celebrated at holy wells and springs, and these natural shrines are resorted to on occasions for which the Church gives no official sanction. Protestant sects also, particularly the more primitive, spiritual ones, invoke the religious spirit by the imagery of rock, well and fountain. In the course of centuries the 'civilized' religions, Christian and Islamic, have failed to replace the primeval worship of the earth spirit by their more expedient moralistic deities, and have had to reconcile themselves to the realities of human and divine nature. So the fact remains, and will remain as long as people survive to recognize it, that a natural affinity exists between the earth and its offspring, both parties being animated by the same spirit and united by common interests.

In the religious symbolism of later times, as in the experience of all people from the beginning, the spirit of the earth energizes in many different forms; and these vary according to one factor, which is the relationship between this receptive 'female' spirit and her mate and polar opposite, the positive 'male' power of the sun. The earliest known man-made images are the hideous, squat representations of the pregnant earth goddess – hideous, that is to the aesthetic eye, to which however these objects were not addressed, having been shaped for a more practical purpose. They are often found in caves and subterranean shrines, and symbolize, obviously enough, the condition of the earth goddess following her union with the god of the heavens. Her other appearances, as virgin, bride, matron and withered hag, correspond to the seasons, and so ultimately to the state of her cosmic relationship. Characteristic of the earth spirit, and in accordance with its feminine nature, is its tendency to withdraw, to decline within the earth's dark recesses. In contrast, the predominant tendency of the positive force is to expand and activate. Thus in nature there are two opposite, complementary principles, the contracting and the expanding, or, in the language of Chinese metaphysics, the yin and the yang, through the interactions of which the balance of the universe and the cycles of life are perpetuated. In their myriad forms yin and yang are manifest throughout creation, but in essence they are unmanifest, being no more than concepts of the divine, as of the human mind. Proceeding from one source, yin-yang is indivisible, the presence of one term implying the other exactly like the negative and positive poles of a magnet. To think of them as sexual opposites is inadequate, for sexuality is but one aspect of their function. The pillar, the mountain, the erect stone, the tall tree are no doubt phallic symbols, but then, as Jung remarked, so is the penis. The phallus they all symbolize is the source of generative power in the universe, humorously represented as the organ of God the Father. This functions perfectly well without human intervention, and the first men were content to observe and accommodate themselves to the moods of the earth spirit as conditioned thereby. It was only later, when the artificial modes of settled life demanded the support of a technology, that the yang force was invoked by the erection of 'phallic' pillars and the deification of the sun.

In 1889 the sturdy radical, Edward Carpenter, published a book with the provocative title, *Civilization: its Cause and Cure,* which in its opening paragraph referred to civilization as 'a kind of disease which the various races of men have to pass through'. The book was attacked by the Socialists of the Fabian Society, and by critics in general, with a degree of venom normally reserved for those heretics who deny the first principles of established religion. And indeed, by the end of the nineteenth century the miraculous wealth created by industry, science and usury, and sanctified by the cosmogony of Darwinism, had elevated the current belief in progress to the status of a religious faith. Carpenter's suggestion that the term 'civilization' be given an historical rather than an ideal value shocked rational people of that time as deeply as the historical approach to Christian legends shocked the old-fashioned clergymen. Since then, of course, ideas have changed: faith in progress is in decline, and it is possible to consider civilization as an historical phenomenon rather than as the divinely appointed goal of human development. Far from being a threat to civilization, this change of attitude could prove to be its salvation, for the most obvious yet neglected feature of the civilized state is its artificiality. Civilization is created by men in defiance of human nature. It is an artifact, made and maintained by art, and if the art is not cultivated it must necessarily decline. It is in the interests of civilization therefore to examine the conditions under which it first arose and the methods that have been used to preserve it.

The origins of civilization are prehistoric, of an age beyond literary record, so the only accessible source of information is the record of 'sacred history', which differs from the profane variety in that it reaches vastly further back into the past, drawing its material from myth and traditional cosmogony. Changes in the order of human society are represented in sacred history as changes in the hierarchy of gods. Thus the first revolution of Olympus marks the first deviation from the primeval ways of men. The golden age in Greek mythology was presided over by Cronus, otherwise Saturn. He was a most conservative ruler, determined to preserve the stability of his realm without change, and this he achieved by devouring all the children born to his wife, Rhea, daughter of Earth and Sky, for it was prophesied that he would one day be overthrown by a son. The time came when Rhea grew tired of this habit, and when she bore Zeus, she hid him in a cave in Crete, giving the father in place of the baby a wrapped stone. In due course Cronus was overcome by Zeus and retired, according to Hesiod, to the Fortunate Isles or, in Plutarch's account, to an island off the coast of Britain (one of the Scilly Isles is indicated), where in the manner of eclipsed gods and heroes he sleeps in the company of his retainers. So Cronus gave way to Zeus, and to a pantheon of earth and sky deities, in a revolution signifying a corresponding revolution in human affairs and a change in the relationship of gods and men. The wandering tribes of the age of Cronus, the simple hunters and food gatherers, had new gods to preside over new activities. Technology began with the theft by Prometheus of the artificer's fire; Hestia, goddess of the hearth, encouraged the habit of settlement, and the old cyclical life of nomadism gave way to a pastoral, agricultural economy.

There is of course much to be gained materially from this development, but the difficulty is that human nature has been formed, or at least deeply conditioned by millennia of existence dominated by the rhythms of the earth goddess and the heavenly bodies. Settlement involves loss of contact with the divinities that had ruled all previous time, removes from life its deepest reality and certainty, frustrates human nature. Men become as Adam expelled from the Garden of Eden. It is their immediate concern, having eaten of the tree of knowledge, to apply all their newly acquired arts to constructing a facsimile of the Garden, a model paradise, containing all the elements in their previous experience. So all settlements develop as cosmological schemes, representing in microcosm the order of the heavens as corresponding to the order of life and the pattern of the human mind. The marks people make on the ground reflect the philosophy of the time. Before the rise of philosophy in compensation for the inadequacies of civilized life, the earth is preserved unchanged as it left the hands of its maker; every later development of philosophy is faithfully depicted by men on its surface, whether consciously or not. The groves and temples of Arcadia, the radiating avenues of the imperial centre, the neatly ordered municipal garden, and the spoils and effluents of industrial rapacity, are each the product of a certain cosmology, a certain view of the nature of the universe and its relationship to men. On the face of the landscape can be seen the effects of the former sacred view of the earth and of the contrasting view now prevailing.

The philosophy that goes with the life-style of the wandering man is that of Heraclitus: 'All is in flow.' Every river is as sacred as the Ganges, according to the Indian saying; for the earth is pervaded by spirit in all its parts, and the nomad's garden of paradise extends over its entire surface. The prospect of the settled man is more limited. His territory is confined to his neighbourhood. In giving up the wandering life he has deprived himself of the full range of experience demanded by human nature, and in compensation he tries to reproduce on a small scale the sacred landscape of his ancestors. His formal paradise, which takes the place of the real thing, is consciously sanctified; the gods, localized in shrines, are invoked at their proper seasons by magic and ritual, their natural accessibility having lapsed. Whereas formerly every part of the earth was inhabited and directly ruled by spirits, these are now placed in reservations that the world outside may be freed for the sacrilegious proceeding of breaking the earth for agriculture, building and mining. Even so, these activities are carried out in the knowledge that they are objectionable to the earth spirit and defy the gods. They must therefore be attended by ritual designed to attract the gods' patronage. The farmer's year is regulated by the old deities, sun and moon, and its stages are sanctified by festivals and sacrifice; the sites of tombs, temples, houses and all artificial features of the landscape are located in relation to the paths and centres of the earth spirit, with placatory sacrifice at their foundation; mining, a particularly bold undertaking, demands a most circumspect approach to the earth spirit, details of which are given in Mircea Eliade's *The Forge and the Crucible*, involving ritual purification of the miners and magic ceremonies to gain the sympathy of the gods. The life of nomadic people, governed by the strict laws of nature, proceeds in ritual fashion, and the ritual cycle of the year thus produced is repeated in settled communities, the difference being that whereas it was formerly spontaneous, among settled people it proceeds according to the word of the priest.

Settlement leads to the establishment of social hierarchies, to specialization, the development of arts and sciences, the building of temples and houses. For millions of years men, essentially the same as we are now, lived without these and presumably without feeling the need for them. Unlike many animals, men are not equipped by nature with the instinct to build houses. In the words of the New Testament, 'The foxes have holes and the birds of the air have nests; but the son of man hath not where to lay his head', and there are still people who are content to live accordingly. Tacitus describes a German tribe that lived entirely without artificial shelter, and another so proud that its members scorned to have personal possessions. Even today in frozen Patagonia the Ona people live out of doors, though, as Lord Raglan points out, they make ceremonial shrines for the gods. How and when the first settlements came about is a mystery; but as caves were residences of the earth spirit before they were inhabited by men, so it appears that the first buildings were temples and only later houses. It is significant that the earliest town known to archaeology, Jericho, was founded at the site of a sacred spring, and the original structure of about 8000 BC, lying beneath many layers of debris from later buildings, has been identified as a shrine to the local spirit. Towns may come and go, says the *I Ching*, but the well remains where it always was, thus explaining the phenomenon of successive towns built round the same sacred place, the spirit of which became the foundation deity, receiving the sacrifices offered in expiation of the crime of settlement and giving the law by which the city was governed. Implicit in this law was a contract between man and god by which the first was permitted a conditional use of land for agriculture and building in return for duties and observances paid to the second. So it was understood by the founding fathers of ancient cities. But as cities expand these limitations become more onerous and more neglected, with the result that, in the language of apocalypse, the holy city becomes Babylon, the parasitic whore, and proceeds to destruction. In this belief, the conservative element in ancient Rome objected to imperial expansion beyond the original city boundaries, considering it a breach of the foundation contract. Such counsels were of course ignored, and in consequence Rome, following the career of all previous empires, became Babylon indeed.

Plato, with his cyclical view of history, believed that civil life has been going on for 'a vast and incredible length of time' during which 'many thousands of cities have come into being and the same number have come to an end'. According to this view the tendency to form settlements is recurrent, with civilizations developing through-out history and collapsing, either, like the Tower of Babel, through the folly and arrogance of their inhabitants or, like Atlantis, through natural disasters. This traditional view of history is at present unfashionable, but there are in fact good indications that developed civilizations have existed in remote antiquity. Perhaps the most convincing to anyone who cares to study the subject is the existence all over the world of traditional units of measure that are undoubtedly derived, like the modern metre, from significant fractions of the earth's dimension or, as in the case of the unit still surviving as the English mile, from an ancient canon of cosmology (details of which are given in the present writer's *City of Revelation*), a canon which provided the ground plan of temples from at least as early as the building of Stonehenge to Christian times. An example cited in A. E. Berriman's *Historical Metrology* is the Greek furlong, of which there are exactly 216,000 in the earth's polar circumference, the number 216,000 being equal to 60 × 60 × 60 and thus an important number in the Sumerian sexagesimal system which has given us the 360-degree division of the circle and the 60-minute hour. The fact is that the exact sciences as practised in ancient Egypt, Greece and Rome were less complete than those of earlier times; and they were less widely known. It is evident that the civilizations of historical antiquity derived the better part of their scientific knowledge from the traditions of a more developed, unified and widely disseminated system belonging to a previous age unknown to history. The very same conclusion emerges from the study of certain medieval mariners' maps by Professor C. H. Hapgood, described in his *Maps of the Ancient Sea Kings*. The map of the Turkish admiral Piri Re'is, for example, dated 1513 and copied from earlier charts of the time of Alexander the Great, shows with their correct longitudes details of the South American coast unknown in Europe at the time the map was drawn. Other maps accurately represent parts of the Antarctic continent that have long been covered with ice. Of a twelfth-century Chinese map Professor Hapgood writes: 'It seems to me that the evidence of this map points to the existence in very ancient times of a *world-wide* civilization, the map-makers of which mapped virtually the entire globe with a uniform general level of technology, with similar methods, equal knowledge of mathematics, and probably the same sorts of instruments.'

This of course is not in accordance with modern theories of history, but it does strengthen the theory of Atlantis, the 'ante-diluvian world' that preceded and inspired all subsequent civilizations. So far, for lack of archaeological proof, the debate between the friends and opponents of Atlantis has tended to proceed in political or religious terms, with those who believe in cyclical history accepting Plato's account and those who favour the evolutionary view rejecting it. Modern historians are naturally prone to judge the civilized standards of ancient societies by reference to our own; yet the evidence of Stonehenge and other megalithic sites shows the existence 4,000 years ago of advanced scientific knowledge combined with a natural, unobtrusive technology, suggesting that the present world civilization is not the first, merely the most materially developed and materialistically directed.

The advice given in Plato's *Republic* to settlers in a new country is that they should first discover the shrines and sacred places of the local deities and reconsecrate them to the corresponding principles in the colonists' religion, with festivals instituted on the appropriate days; there should be at least 365 festivals in the course of the year. This was the universal practice of antiquity, and the idea behind it was to create a model of the golden age by imitating the festive cycle of the ancestral nomads. So comes about the continuity of sacred sites in association with a sacred calendar which persists in every religion. And the sanctity of local shrines extends to the paths that lead up to and between them. The god approaches his shrine by a particular route. Once he was accompanied by his celebrants, the wandering tribe that had followed him from his previous residence. Now he comes with a religious procession, a ritualized sacred journey in imitation of the old ways. The celebration of the Mysteries at Eleusis was preceded by a day-long procession during which the pilgrims followed the style of the golden age with simple offerings of local produce at shrines along the way, every one of which had associations with the story of the resident goddess Demeter. In the same spirit, the Australian natives make ritual journeys in the steps of the gods who created the landscape, every feature of which commemorates some episode in cosmogony and has also some present significance for human or animal life. A rock may mark a source of fertility in women, a tree the place from which a certain animal or plant is generated. Each station on the journey has its day of the year, its mythological episode, the rituals and songs appropriate to it and its properties useful to men or animals.

The ways between these places have similar associations, for they are ways of the earth spirit, not merely secular routes but natural channels of energy, first traced out by the creative gods, followed by the primeval wandering tribes and still in settled times used by religious processions or pilgrims to a shrine. Traditionally they are also paths of psychic activity, of apparitions, spirits of the dead or fairies, particularly on one day of the year. People of the Irish countryside recognize certain lines, unmarked on the ground, as fairy paths, lines of a seasonal flow of spirit, which must on no account be obstructed or built on. A house on one of these lines would bring misfortune to its occupants and to the neighbourhood and for the same reason a site between two raths or sacred hilltop enclosures is also avoided. The photograph reproduced on p. 89, showing the corner of an Irish house cut off to allow the passage of a fairy path, is from a book of modern fairy lore, *The Middle Kingdom* by Dermot McManus, containing several instances of the mysterious moving lights associated with these paths. In Celtic tradition they are the spirits of the dead, the will-o'-the-wisps or 'corpse candles' that are said to hover over certain old tracks leading to the local church.

Even among the Anglo-Saxons, supposed to be less perceptive of spiritual phenomena than their Celtic neighbours, the tradition of spirit paths continues in the present generation, as is illustrated by the numerous modern accounts of stretches of haunted tracks recorded in Kathleen Wiltshire's *Ghosts and Legends of the Wiltshire Countryside*. Almost every old religious centre and manor house is locally reputed to be linked to others by a network of secret tracks or underground tunnels. 'We have plenty of evidence to show that the legend of an underground passage indicates a *real* secret route *above* ground', writes Dr Winifred Haward, and in her book *Hide or Hang*, which is about secret rooms and tunnels in the North of England, she records among other such legends the belief that a ghostly 'white lady' follows the course of a supposed secret tunnel from Barnburgh Hall in Yorkshire to St Helen's Chapel nearby. This apparition would in Wales be identified as Elen or Helena, the Celtic goddess of ancient tracks, in whom is remembered the first of all deities, the wandering spirit of the earth. The same is the Greek Hermes, protector of travellers, whose ways were marked by lines of pillars leading to the central stone in the market place; and in Cornwall the old sacred ways are similarly marked by menhirs and stone crosses.

All these various traditions, which occur universally and evidently derive from some once unified system of knowledge about the ways of the earth spirit, refer to, as it were, a stream of magnetic current, fertilizing, and accompanied by manifestations of spirit, that passes through the country on certain routes and on certain days, its seasons determined by the positions of the heavenly bodies. The shrines located on its path were resorted to on those occasions when the local god, representing a particular aspect of the earth spirit, was in temporary residence. The properties of springs, lakes and rivers, says Ovid in the *Metamorphoses,* vary with the seasons. In its early history the oracle at Delphi was active only once a year, and so it is with all natural centres of the earth spirit. Each one has its peculiar season of efficacy, commemorated in the date of the annual fair, feast, market or assembly that has always been held there. By these events were regulated the stages of the agricultural year, and thus the lives of all people in traditional societies proceed according to a sacred calendar, related to local topography, to local myths and customs, and deriving ultimately from people's actual experience of the earth spirit and their recognition of its ways, seasons and centres of influence. Strangers may conquer the land, imposing their own gods and cults on the natives, but the sacred places and the dates of their festivals remain the same as before, the attributes of the new deities are accommodated to the old, and the invaders become in time subject to the traditions of the country. It was the policy of the early Christians to follow antique precedent in this respect, with the result that almost every old church occupies a site with sacred associations far earlier than the present building, while the feast day of the saint to whom the church is dedicated has in many cases been inherited from the god of the previous religion. This continuity in the shrines and seasons of the earth spirit has an economic as well as a mystical cause, for the life of the country is little affected by political or religious change; the seasons of the agricultural year proceed in the same way, and must still be marked by festivals at the regular dates and places, whatever the system of government may be. It is only in recent times that lands have been colonized without the new inhabitants taking over the sacred calendar and topography of the old; and the effect of this omission may be judged by comparing the secularized landscape of, for example, much of North America with that of other continents, where even now most communities are located at sites originally chosen with some consideration for the earth spirit and retain some connection with the past through the associations of the sacred places at which they were founded. The difference between a modern industrial landscape, created by a society in which commercial values are paramount, and the traditional variety which has been developed for a more permanent function and on more permanent principles, illustrates visually the difference between modern and ancient philosophy. In the first case the buildings have been designed and sited for the immediate exploitation of the earth's resources in the interests of material gain with little concern for human nature and none for the proper relationship between the living and the dead. In the second, the earth is regarded as a living creature, whose life, health and fertility are bound up with those of its inhabitants. According to this way of thought, the spirit of the earth and the spirit that animates all living things are of the same essence, so that the interests of men, not only for one life but for all times, are best served by studying the interests of spirit. The practical result of this policy is most clearly apparent in the landscape of China, where for thousands of years, throughout all revolutions and changes of dynasty, the same attitude toward the earth spirit and the same methods of reconciling its ways to the ways of men have been maintained. For the purposes of settled life, these methods were codified in the scientific and magical system of geomancy known as feng-shui, literally 'wind and water', which, since it appears once to have been practised over the entire world, and claims to have eternal and universal application, deserves more serious attention than it has yet attracted from western scholars. This it will no doubt receive when the symptoms of terrestrial sickness have become too blatant to be further ignored and the need arises to consider again the terms of the contract between men and gods by which settlement and civilization are permitted to continue.

The ancient, once universal geomantic science of landscape (feng-shui) can exist only in association with the traditional style of philosophy referred to above, according to which the earth is a living entity animated by spirit. This spirit is the natural environment of the spirits of the dead, and it is also related to the spiritual nature of men. Like the energies of the human body, the spirit of the earth flows through the surface in channels or veins, and between the two energy currents of man and earth there exists a natural affinity that enables men to divine the presence and local character of the earth spirit, to intuit how best to bring human ways into harmony with it, and even, by the exercise of will and imagination, to influence its flow.

Another condition that must obtain wherever geomancy is practised is that the prevailing cosmological idea express the concept of an organic, 'steady state' universe, that has been considered orthodox throughout far the greater part of history, rather than the modern evolutionary 'expanding universe' theory. The first of these two contrasting world views, the traditional one, emphasizes the permanent aspects of human life on earth, the fact that men are always subject to the same laws of the universe and of their own nature. Under these conditions the purpose of science is to benefit the life of the people as it is, and as it essentially always must be so long as the sources of life on earth remain the same. Thus the intention and effect of feng-shui in China was, as Professor Abercrombie puts it, 'to produce a landscape which had to preserve certain spiritual values and also to fulfil the practical purpose of supporting a dense population'. The Chinese were suspicious of all new ideas that were not relevant to this purpose and, observing that such innovations are commonly proposed for their own convenience by the commercial class, they discouraged that class from gaining the power to impose their own values on the others. A further safeguard was that, should a merchant become rich and established, so as to want to imitate the style of his betters, the example he found accepted as the most prestigious mode of life was that of the retired scholar. The modern and opposite tendency is to value artificial above natural sources of wealth, to respect innovations as tokens of human inventiveness, to identify commercial interests with the interests of the people as a whole, and to blame the latter for any resistance to the social change promoted by the former. A high local population is now considered to be a destructive rather than a creative force relative to the harmony and productivity of the landscape; and so, alienated from the earth spirit and the local gods, it has become. In terms of the present system of philosophy, the geomancer's two aims, to preserve the landscape of the golden age and to make it support a large settled population, seem incompatible, which indeed they must be as long as that system prevails.

Feng-shui has been defined as 'the art of adapting the residences of the living and the dead so as to cooperate and harmonize with the local currents of the cosmic breath'. Joseph Needham in *Science and Civilization in China* gives a good concise account of its function:

'Every place had its special topographical features which modified the local influence (hsing shih) of the various ch'i of Nature. The forms of hills and the directions of watercourses, being the outcome of the moulding influences of winds and waters, were the most important, but, in addition, the heights and forms of buildings, and the directions of roads and bridges, were potent factors. The force and nature of the invisible currents would be from hour to hour modified by the positions of the heavenly bodies, so that their aspects as seen from the locality in question had to be considered. While the choosing of sites was of prime importance, bad siting was not irremediable, as ditches and tunnels could be dug, or other measures taken to alter the feng-shui situation. . . .

'The two currents, Yang and Yin, in the earth's surface, were identified with the two symbols which apply to the eastern and western quarters of the sky, the Green Dragon (Chhing Lung) of spring in the former case, the White Tiger (Pai Hu) of autumn in the latter. Each of these would be symbolized by configurations of the ground. The former ought always to be to the left, and the latter to the right, of any tomb or habitation, which should preferably be protected by them, as if in the crook of an elbow. But this was only the beginning of the complexity, since high and abrupt escarpments were considered Yang, and rounded elevations Yin. Such influences (shan ling) had to be balanced, if possible, in the selection of the site, so as to obtain three-fifths Yang and two-fifths Yin.'

Needham goes on to credit feng-shui with 'the great beauty of the siting of so many farms, houses and villages throughout China'.

The long continuity of Chinese civilization, to which feng-shui has made an important contribution, has in turn preserved the methods of that science up to the present day; and thus has come down to us a legacy from the primeval golden age. Not that the early wandering people needed any formal system of feng-shui, because, as they lived and moved under the direct influence of the earth's subtle energies, its principles were naturally integrated in their lives. Like all sciences, feng-shui is an expedient of civilization, a technique for reconciling human nature to the limitations imposed on it by settlement. But the perception of the geomancer is that of an earlier age, the perception of the earth spirit as the ruling factor in life. It is his responsibility to ensure that no changes are made to the shape and appearance of the landscape that might disturb locally the harmonious flow of the earth's vital energy. More than that, he may actually improve the landscape, manifesting its latent powers and making the pattern of its energy field conform more closely to the ideal requirements of its inhabitants. This he does by judicious siting of all buildings, tombs, walls and roads, with the addition of pillars, temples and monuments at the spots designed by nature to receive them. Here is Ernst Börschmann's description of the Chinese landscape as formed by feng-shui from the text of his fine book of photographs, *Picturesque China*:

'Certain summits of the neighbouring mountains, often the main summit, are crowned with pagodas, small temples or pavilions to harmonize the magic forces of heaven and earth. This thought is akin, for instance, to our conception of the outflow of magnetic force from a pointed conductor. And the Chinese geomancer also regards the forms of nature as a magnetic field.'

The field of terrestrial magnetism, like the energy field of a plant or animal, exists only by association with a living body; and as traditional Chinese medicine by acupuncture treats the human body by regulating the currents of vital energy that flow through the skin, so the geomancer treats the body of the earth. Textbooks of feng-shui describe the nature of the telluric current, give examples of the energy patterns it forms in relation to different kinds of landscape and landscape features, and show ways of adapting its natural flow to human convenience. In some districts, particularly in wild, steep, rocky parts, the ways of the earth spirit are rapid and violent, and if the country is to be made habitable its energy must be tamed and directed into more evenly flowing channels. Where, as in flat, featureless country, it moves too sluggishly, with a tendency to stagnate, it can be stimulated by making lengths of straight avenues and watercourses and adding vertical features to the landscape. Thus the irregular fissures in which streams of energy cascade down the mountains are picked up and domesticated in the valleys by the stone walls of the fields surrounding a settlement, and an inspired example of feng-shui principles in England is the tall spire of Salisbury Cathedral (a building said to have been sited by divination on the spot marked by the fall of an arrow shot from the hill of Old Sarum), rising above the water meadows of the Avon. In feng-shui the laws of dynamics and aesthetics are united by the one canon that serves both, resulting in a landscape delightful to the eye of poet and philosopher and best disposed to fulfil the practical requirements of the people.

An important factor in manipulating the earth's subtle energies is the influence of the heavenly bodies, particularly the sun and moon, which throughout the day, varying with their respective positions, set up tides and currents within the terrestrial magnetic field. So the patterns on earth follow the patterns in the heavens, and the geomancer's task in shaping the landscape is to emphasize this correspondence. His professional qualifications combine a knowledge of the traditional sciences, astronomy, astrology, geometry, number and proportion and land surveying, with the diviner's direct sensitivity to the flow of telluric energies. His instrument is the magnetic compass, first used, according to Needham, for purposes of feng-shui. The geomancer's compass is set in the middle of a circular wooden board inscribed with a number of concentric circles, each ring divided into segments marked with letters and symbols, from which the geomancer can read off the properties of any piece of ground and the influences it is subject to, thereby discovering whether or not it is an auspicious site for the purpose he has in mind. There is a detailed interpretation of the various sets of symbols on the geomancer's compass in E. J. Eitel's *Feng-Shui*, a curious book, published a hundred years ago and now again in print, by a prim clergyman of the London Missionary Society in China. As a representative of western civilization, Eitel had naturally to compare Chinese science unfavourably with the European system, but despite this, he gives a sympathetic account of feng-shui as a force that spared the Chinese landscape from the excesses of nineteenth-century industrialization. It is, he writes, 'eagerly availed of by ministers of state as a satisfactory excuse for their own unwillingness to further the progress of trade and civilization'. Yet he continues, 'Would God that our own men of science had preserved . . . that child-like reverence for the living powers of nature, that sacred awe and trembling fear of the mysteries of the unseen, that firm belief in the realities of the invisible world and its constant intercommunication with the seen and the temporal, which characterize these Chinese gropings after natural science.'

A use of feng-shui that became ever more important with the growth of the Chinese empire was to assist the concentration of power in the imperial capital by diverting the natural, serpentine streams of earth energy into long straight channels and directing them towards the emperor at the seat of government in Peking. These channels were the imperial dragon paths (lung mei) of China, carefully preserved even into the present century by the Government Board of Rites; on their course no buildings or tombs other than those of the emperor and his family were allowed to be sited. Some stretches were paved and became used as roads; others ran invisibly across country, their course marked by obelisks, ceremonial bridges and temples with their main axes coinciding with the alignment. In this way the spiritual energies of the earth, generated in mountain temples and monasteries, their flow regulated at sacred stations along the way, sustained the emperor, as he was also sustained by the service of the people. By the same channels, the solar current, distilled from above by the emperor and his hierarchical, cosmologically ordered court, diffused its fertilizing influence throughout the kingdom.

As well as having this symbolic and magical function, straight roads running to all parts of the country from the imperial centre have also, of course, a more obvious use to the state rulers as providing means of control and communication. And thus the mystical, as always, combines with the practical. Hitler observed that empires are built on straight roads, and through his architect, Albert Speer, arranged the ceremonial centres at the foundation of the Third Reich accordingly. The influence of Rome was extended throughout its empire by a network of roads conceived as radiating from the centre; so was the power of the pre-Conquest empires of Central and South America. Versailles, with its avenues directed towards the seat of the Sun King, is the complete image of the imperial solar capital. In England, the great sixteenth-century landowners cut or planted long rides that stretched from their palaces to distant towers and castles often far beyond their own possessions, thus symbolizing and magically procuring control over the surrounding countryside. This arrangement was also convenient for the noble occupation of stag hunting, and to that extent the long woodland avenues had their mundane purpose; but essentially their function was mystical, to set up a two-way flow of spirit between the local ruler and the people, with the palace as the control centre and point of fusion. Many other architectural features, now commonly considered only in their practical aspect, have similar mystical origins, beginning as devices for feng-shui purposes. Mircea Eliade writes: 'It is highly probable that the fortifications of inhabited places and cities began by being magical defences; for fortifications – trenches, labyrinths, ramparts, etc – were designed to repel invasions by demons and the souls of the dead rather than attacks by human beings.' The Great Wall of China served an obvious military purpose, but it was also built in accordance with feng-shui principles, to shelter the kingdom from the unfavourable influences traditionally located in the north. Whether these were manifest through invading armies of men or demons was of little practical consequence. The Wall excluded both, in the same way that a wall round a park or garden preserves both its physical inviolability and its peaceful atmosphere.

Feng-shui, as the Chinese acknowledge, is or has been practised universally. Its simple origin, as a method by which wandering people divine the course of the earth spirit, is illustrated in Spencer and Gillen's account of the Achilpa, a tribe of Australian nomads, who carry with them a wooden pole and take whatever direction is indicated by the way in which the pole bends. So there are people among us today who make every decision in life by reference to a pendulum, horoscope or home oracle. When one of the Achilpa clans broke its pole, its members became distraught, lay on the ground and waited for death. At the other extreme are the highly technical systems of feng-shui which, as civilizations grow more elaborate, have been developed to support them. In the empires of antiquity it was a state-controlled science, directed by the emperor himself, whose main responsibility was to observe meticulously the rituals connected with it. Court life was conducted according to the pattern of the heavens, with the king, as the sun in the planetary system, rising at sunrise, retiring at dusk and throughout the seasons imitating the sun in its different aspects. The fourth-century Roman Emperor Julian, who restored for a time the old religion, described himself in his *Oration* as 'attendant of the sovereign Sun', for 'the planets, dancing round him as their king, harmoniously revolve in a circle with definite intervals about his orb, producing certain stable energies'. It is a remarkable tribute to the will and power of the Church to suppress the old cosmology that it was more than a thousand years after Julian that Copernicus began timidly to reintroduce the traditional heliocentric system; and it is a remarkable token of the political influence of cosmology that suppression was considered necessary. In justification of the Christians (who opposed the old magical system at a time when it had become degenerate and, deprived of its former control by responsible temple initiates, dangerous), one need only consider the effects of the old cosmology as, distorted to caricature, misapplied and vulgarly manipulated, it reappeared in Hitler's Reich. Chauvinistic supporters of modern institutions as self-evident improvements on the old may profitably compare this recent travesty with the canonical pattern of kingship that was established throughout the ancient world.

In Ireland, for example, the High King's court at Tara was arranged as a microcosm of the heavens and of the country as a whole, thus imprinting the kingdom with a sacred pattern and declaring as official policy the unsuppressible human ambition for paradise on earth. Assemblies were held, attended by the kings of the four provinces, corresponding to the four points of the compass, together with their followers who occupied the four provincial halls, north, south, east and west, while the kings sat facing their provinces round the High King in the central hall. He was at that moment at the very centre of the universe, setting forth the pattern of cosmic harmony as the model for affairs on earth, and symbolizing the ancient idea that each individual is at the centre of his own universe and is therefore responsible for ordering it on true cosmological principles. Similar events took place at the appointed seasons at provincial and local centres of power. In China there was an important ceremony at the winter solstice, when the Emperor knelt at the centre of the circular walls and terraces of the Temple of Heaven, which constituted a cosmological scheme like the rings on a geomancer's compass. In Edkins's account, 'he thus seems to himself and his court to be in the centre of the universe, and turning to the north, assuming the attitude of a subject, he acknowledges in prayer and by his position that he is inferior to heaven, and to heaven alone'. The sacred king, functioning in the social system as the sun in the planetary, charged with solar energy and transmitting it to the people, was a universal institution, known throughout the East, in the African kingdoms and even as far and as recently as North America in the eighteenth century. At Natchez a solar king reigned from an observatory temple on the great mound, which only he might enter. He was called the Great Sun, dressed in a cloak of feathers, and throughout his reign he never touched the ground, being borne around in a litter for fear he might discharge the solar power invested in him. The Great Sun, his hierarchy of lesser suns, and the beautifully structured society he served, were exterminated by the French in 1729, a few survivors taking refuge among the neighbouring Indians, by whom they were respected for their magical powers.

Such institutions were no doubt highly artificial, but then, as already emphasized, so is civilization. And the solar king was no mere symbol, ornament or tax-eater, but a working instrument, a kind of electric generator or conductor of the positive current by which the spirit of the people and the fertility of the earth itself were maintained. In some cases, if the king did not 'work', if the forces of nature were unresponsive to his influence, he might be deposed. It was a custom of the Assyrians to punish him for any calamity suffered by the people. In China, natural disasters, as well as social disturbances, were attributed to the emperor's carelessness in the performance of ritual, or to wrong relationships within the court, every type of disaster having its particular cause which the emperor was required to remedy. Some of these are specified in 'The Great Law', a chapter in the *Chinese Annals*, edited in 1050 BC and quoted by Raphael Patai in his *Man and Temple*:

'When the course of nature goes its proper way, it is a sign that the government is good, but when there is some disturbance in nature, it is a sign that there is some error in government. With the help of fixed tables it is possible to learn from the disturbance in nature what is the sin that caused it. Any disturbance in the sun accuses the emperor. A disturbance around the sun – the court, the ministers; a disturbance in the moon – the queen, the harem. Good weather that lasts too long shows that the emperor is too inactive. Days which continue to be too cloudy show that the emperor lacks understanding. Too much rainfall shows that he is unjust. Lack of rain shows that he is careless. Stormy wind, that he is lazy. Good harvest proves that everything is all right; bad harvest, that the government is guilty.'

On the other hand, 'the extreme excellence of good government is so fragrant that it influences intelligent and invisible beings'. So it is stated in the *Shu-King*. Here is revealed an essential difference between ancient and modern theories of government: under the former system, disturbances among the people were blamed on errors in government, the assumption being that human nature responds agreeably to cosmic harmony and thus to its faithful reflection in the conduct of the rulers. If that conduct is not in accordance with the heavenly pattern, the people are naturally and rightly rebellious. The modern tendency, promoted by the evolutionists' abolition of human nature as a constant standard, is to establish some secular social theory as state law, require the people to conform to it, and coerce them if they fail to adapt their ways accordingly. As for the 'intelligent and invisible beings', the spirits of earth and the dead, whose interests were considered before all else by the ancient law-givers, under materialism they have no vote and so are not consulted.

Despite the warnings of prophets and the efforts of all sensible people to arrest its progress, civilization tends to grow more elaborate and to make ever greater demands on the earth that sustains it. There comes a time when the old, natural devotion to the earth spirit, together with the traditionalist ideal of preserving the earth as the gods made it, is exchanged for a new object, which is the desire to increase the products of the earth by artificially stimulating its fertility. This stage is marked in sacred history by the appearance of sun gods, the heroic divinities of reason, intellect and centralized government, whose legends refer always to their victories over dragons or serpents, sacred emblems of the previous order. At Delphi, where in archaic times oracles were given in the name of the goddess Earth, the sun god, Apollo, killed Python, the goddess's serpent, and usurped the shrine together with the oracular function. Zeus killed Typhon, the dragon offspring of Earth, and took over the oracle at Dodona, and St Michael, as archangel, kept the hilltop shrines and the reputation as a dragon killer that he had previously enjoyed as a Celtic sun god.

In the terminology of feng-shui the serpent represents the mercurial currents of the earth spirit gliding in serpentine channels through the earth's crust – the yin force in nature. It is to this force that Plutarch, who was a priest at Delphi in the first century AD, refers in *The Decline of Oracles*: 'Men are affected by streams of varying potency issuing from the earth. Some of these drive people crazy or cause disease or death; the effect of others is good, soothing and beneficial.' The factor that produces from the one source these various effects is the complementary yang force, the power of the sun. So Plutarch, in reference to the oracular power of the earth spirit, goes on to quote the old belief that 'the sun creates in the earth the right conditions and the right temperament for it to be able to produce the exhalations that inspire prophecy'. This understanding was the basis of the solar technology that has at different periods brought revolutionary changes into the lives and ideals of people throughout the world.

When the serpent current of the earth spirit is transfixed by the lance of the dragon killer, it can no longer move freely about the earth, for its energies are now fixed and concentrated on one spot. When Apollo killed Python, he performed an act that is repeated in feng-shui ritual wherever the foundation stone of a house or temple is laid. The Indian procedure is described in Eliade's *The Sacred and the Profane*:

'Before the masons lay the first stone, the astronomer shows them the spot where it is to be placed, and this spot is supposed to lie above the snake that supports the world. The master mason sharpens a stake and drives it into the ground, exactly at the indicated spot, in order to fix the snake's head. A foundation stone is then laid above the snake. Thus the cornerstone is at the exact centre of the world.'

St Joseph of Arimathaea is said to have done much the same at the foundation of Christian Glastonbury by planting in the earth his staff which blossomed into the sacred thorn, and there are many similar foundation legends elsewhere. At Delphi, by spearing the serpent and so localizing its energies, Apollo raised the productivity of the oracle, which, having previously been visited by the animating spirit on only one occasion in the year, now became active the year through, except for three months when the god was absent and Dionysus, reigning in his place, temporarily restored the wilder, more elemental rites of the past.

The same policy of artificially increasing the earth's fertility and multiplying the gifts of its spirit, instead of accepting what is given by nature, is evident wherever the solar gods take over the archaic shrines of the earth goddess. The appearance of the sun god signals the introduction of a technology that aims to alter the natural channels of the earth spirit and to stimulate its energies for the benefit of an increasingly large settled population. This innovation is naturally opposed by traditionalists and religious people, and so in the *Eumenides* of Aeschylus the Furies, servants of the old Delphic goddess, cry against Apollo: 'He made man's ways cross the place of the ways of god and blighted age-old distributions of power.'

In the Temple of Apollo at Delphi was the omphalos stone that marked for the Greeks the centre of the world. It was also said to stand over the tomb of Python which implies that it was at the spot where the stake was driven through the head of the serpent at the foundation of the sun god's shrine. Thus it served to concentrate the powerful telluric energies of the place on that one spot and to intensify the local power of the earth spirit to generate prophecy. The 'age-old distributions of power' were disturbed, and the prophetic influence was diverted from the place where it formerly issued, near the Castalian spring and the Sibyl's rock, to the omphalos in Apollo's temple.

In describing the activities carried out by the priests of the sun gods as a technology, it is not intended to suggest that theirs was a mechanical science confined by the laws of physics, but science of a more subtle, metaphysical order. The object of their attention was the animistic world of spirit, the forces of nature called by the Chinese the Kwei Shin and known by various names to all people on earth. The attributes of this dualistic spirit, the Kwei and the Shin, are yin and yang respectively, the first signifying the contracting principle as exhibited in the Lares Rustici, the nymphs of hills and streams, the grosser spirits of the dead, the second being the expansive force, the spirits of the upper air and the finer part of the spirit in men. These two have to some extent different characteristics, the Kwei for instance responding to ritual while the Shin are properly invoked by music; but in practice they are inseparable, complementary opposites of the same order, and in magical ceremony they are addressed together as the Kwei Shin.

Spirits are invoked in temples, each one of which is unique because it is designed to attract a particular god or aspect of a god and must therefore feature his peculiar local attributes. Men in their natural state do not invoke gods, being content with what is given unasked by nature; and to do so, to study the Kwei Shin, to note their ways, weaknesses and potentialities, and to use this knowledge in the construction of shrines for localizing their energies, is a form of technology that has been refined to a point of great precision in the past. Archaeologists have to some extent succeeded in reconstructing the physical life-style of the people who covered great areas of northern Europe with their monumental apparatus of stone circles, pillars and dolmens some four or five thousand years ago, but for the monuments themselves they have no explanation, apart from vague suggestions of a ritual purpose in connection with a cult of the dead. This is indeed so, but astronomers now recognize that all these great stones, from the vast, extensive alignments of Carnac and the sun-moon temple of Stonehenge to remote sites in the northern isles of Scotland, were precisely located in relation to the heavenly bodies and the natural features of the landscape. From all that has recently been discovered about the scientific knowledge and methods of the megalith builders, it appears that their system was in the synthetic magical tradition of Egypt, Babylon and the ancient East; and it was certainly in close accordance with the principles of feng-shui, for the same astronomical and geological factors that the Chinese geomancers considered in locating the sites of temples and tombs are also apparent as having determined the sites of the corresponding monuments in Europe. For many years now, experienced dowsers, including Merle and Diot in France and Guy Underwood, Reginald Smith and many others in Britain, have observed the fact that every megalithic site is over a centre or channel of the terrestrial current whose emanations are detected by the dowser's rod. All ancient tombs and stones were placed so as to coincide with and accumulate the flow of the earth's vital energy, its 'spirit'; and this implies that the 'cult of the dead', which all agree was an important motivation of the great stone builders, was not merely the pious and superstitious hope of life eternal that savages are supposed to cherish and Christians often do, but a very exact science of spiritual invocation, of such proven value, in terms of benefits obtained, that by the beginning of the second millenium BC the greater part of the physical and intellectual resources of nations throughout Europe must have been devoted to its maintenance. The very number and size of prehistoric works in earth and stone; their occurrence, together with the habitations of their human contemporaries, in the remote islands and desolate parts of Europe which no one now either cares to or knows how to populate: these alone give some picture of the numerous and widely distributed population that was supported by the subtle technology of the great stone builders in western Europe, as it was by feng-shui in China. 'They grew corn on the sides of hills which we now never attempt to stir,' said William Cobbett in his early nineteenth-century travels, as he observed the ramparts and terraces of neolithic cultivators all over the deserted downlands of southern England; and as final evidence of the high spirit engendered by the ancient science one need only compare the present melancholy, depopulated condition of the highlands and western coast districts of Britain and Europe with those same parts as they must have been when inhabited by the ancient people whose heroic level of experience is revealed in the myths and bardic traditions that have survived them, and whose magical achievements persist in the folklore associated with their monuments.

A remarkable relic from the prehistoric past is the body of local tradition, consistent throughout Europe and beyond, that attributes to every ancient stone and sacred place certain of the various qualities that are traditionally functions of the earth spirit. In the many cases where megalithic structures have been erected by or above sacred springs or at other such natural shrines, it is obvious that their local reputation as instruments of healing or fertility or as centres of spiritual activity has been taken over by them from the ground on which they stand. Thus a stone placed by a healing well may serve as a permanent residence, like a storage battery, for the spirit that formerly animated the water only for a short season in the year. Every ancient standing stone is like the omphalos in the Temple of Apollo, driven into the head of the telluric serpent current, fixing and augmenting the energies which had formerly fluctuated. Yet in the end the system became onerous and ineffective, demanding at least as much from the people as it gave in return. St Patrick is said to have freed Ireland from the final excesses of a degenerate priesthood, whose altars demanded ever more sacrificial blood before they could evoke response from the resident spirits. The Celtic saints aimed to restore the earlier invocations of the earth spirit at its natural springs rather than in the temples and stone monuments where their ancestors had located them, and their attitude survives in the spiritual, nonconformist sects of the modern Celts, deriving from the Protestant Reformation.

Why this should have happened, why the spirits located in stones and temples should have abandoned them or become unsusceptible to invocation, is a question that deeply concerned the Greeks of classical times. Plato referred to the denser population and higher fertility of the country in past ages, when the native spirit was animated and everywhere streams of prophecy issued from the oracles. By the beginning of the Christian era, the oracles, which had long been corrupt, were almost all extinct. Many people believed that the gods were dying in portent of the approaching end of the world. Plutarch put forward an alternative, less hysterical theory to account for the withdrawal of the earth spirit from its old familiar shrines, that 'with regard to the powers that are associated with the earth, it is quite likely that these should change their locations, that their flow, impelled from some other direction, should alter its course and that within the earth there should be in the whole course of time many revolutions from such cyclical processes. . . . And the same view should certainly be accepted with regard to the spirits of prophecy; their power should not be thought of as eternal and ageless, but as subject to change.'

Here is revealed the inevitable betrayal by any institutionalized system of technology of the people who have come to depend on it. The earth spirit, as Plutarch indicates, is only apparently constant in its seasonal tides, for over great periods – and sometimes abruptly because of earthquakes, cataclysm, etc – its course shifts, as do the beds of rivers. In this it follows the slow orbital variations of the heavenly bodies. The early nomadic people, living by and imitating the ways of the earth spirit, could adapt themselves to its gradual changes. The settled people, however, wanted their gods to settle with them, and so located them in shrines to be visited at seasons determined by the priest's calendar; and finally these shrines were adorned with temples as permanent residences of spirit. The land became more productive, the people richer and more numerous – until, under the influence of cyclical changes in the heavens, the flow of spirit began to withdraw from the temples and take other paths. The latter-day priests, having neglected the principles of the old astronomical science by which the temples were first sited and planned, and no longer sensitive to the earth's spiritual energies, could only resort to more frantic invocations, attended by ever increasing sacrifice, in attempts to repeat the former results. And thus followed, as it has on many occasions and at many places over the world, a reaction against the artificial and ever more futile proceedings of the magicians, and a return to simpler ways.

In this brief account of developments in the eternal relationship between men and earth, the principal reference has been to the earth's spirit, called by such various synonyms as the 'serpent current', the 'telluric force' and 'the earth's subtle energies'. Its names are legion. It is the prana or mana of eastern metaphysics, the 'vril', the 'universal plastic medium', of occultists, the anima mundi of alchemy. Its modern 'discoverers' have each given it names of their own: animal magnetism, odyle, orgone energy. Dr Wilhelm Reich tried to catch it in boxes of wood and metal; the playwright August Strindberg hunted it with a bottle of liquid lead acetate in the cemetery of Montparnasse. Its properties have been discussed for as long as there have been people capable of discussing anything, and so wide and contradictory is the range of its manifestations that the epithets applied to it have varied from 'Satan, that old serpent' to 'Bride of Christ'. To the ancients it was notoriously two-faced, and this quality is reflected in the gods that personify its many aspects. As Mercurius it has an affinity with all animated spirit, for that god 'runs round the world enjoying alike the company of the good and wicked'. He is a god of both life and death, of initiation, inspiration, prophecy and delusion, the traveller's friend, yet to his earnest, uncritically devoted followers a wilful deceiver and 'fool's lantern'. His company is kept by the high-spirited of all temperaments, and the course of his study is a popular path to madness.

Like Kundalini, the vital serpent current that animates living bodies, the spirit of the earth is discernible only in its effects and not by analysis. It is therefore of no concern to physical science and may not be included in the scientific canon of existent phenomena. Yet its influence was formerly considered to condition every aspect of life on earth, and, as already here indicated, heroic efforts have been made by individuals, as well as by the priests and scientists of great states, to learn its secrets so as to bring forth its more socially desirable properties. The alchemists aimed to capture the spirit of Mercurius as the mobile agent in their operations, and they spoke of 'fixing' it, using the imagery of the stake driven through the earth serpent, by which means their predecessors, alchemists of elemental cosmic forces, had attempted to raise the subtle spirit of the earth.

All these good people shared the noblest ambition, to invoke again the golden age on earth. No doubt in their time they did much to promote human convenience and comfort, and civilizations have been humanized by such efforts; but their falls have thereby only been delayed. For the human spirit, like the spirit of the earth, is a natural wanderer and does not for ever accept domesticity. Attempts to fix nature's volatile principle will always be made; and the spirit may for a time accept the ways imposed on it by human nature in its material aspect. But sooner or later it will prefer its own ways, and will take them, whatever obstacles are put in its path. Behind this animated current is the Mystery, hinted at in the catacombs of Eleusis, that may not fully be comprehended within the natural limits of human experience. Thus is feng-shui translated as 'wind and water', because, as the Reverend E. J. Eitel was told by his Chinese houseboy, 'it's a thing like wind which you can not comprehend, and like water which you can not grasp'.

1 A sacred imprint on landscape. The Celtic cross, universal symbol of the perfect harmony of the cosmos, is discovered from the air lying at the foundations of this Mexican fishing village and so revealing the true philosophy of its founders. (Fishing village in a lagoon, Pacific coast, Mexico.)

2, 3, 4 A Chinese geomancer's compass is the instrument by which he determines the correct site for every tomb, temple and house and the correct use for every piece of land, thus preserving the flow of the earth's subtle currents and directing the work of men in accordance with the interests of nature. The rings on the disc relate to the points of the compass, astrological influences and local landscape features. The beautiful, productive and densely populated landscape of old China was a creation of the geomancer's art. (2 Mountain landscape, painting by K'ung Ts'an, China, 17th century; 3 The Imperial Travelling Palace at the Hoo-Kew-Shan, from a sketch by Thomas Allom, *China Illustrated, c.* 1840; 4 Chinese geomantic compass.)

Preceding page:
5 The famous Ohio earthwork depicting the serpent and the egg, a universal symbol of the alchemical science. This is one of the many animal effigy mounds made by the ancient American Indians which can be interpreted only from the air. (Serpent Mound, near Locust Grove, Ohio, USA.)

6 The earth and the abundance of nature are represented by the image of a fertile woman, the result of creative union between the forces of heaven and earth. The image, a magical object, is intended to procure in reality the state it symbolizes. As the child is conceived in the womb, so is the spirit of the earth engendered within the subterranean depths. (Neolithic figurine from Tel Chagar Bazar, Mesopotamia.)

7 The verses (right) translated from the seventeenth-century Latin of Stolcius refer to the grand and oldest branch of alchemy, which was concerned to bring about the earthly paradise through the fruitful union of cosmic and terrestrial forces. The principles of early alchemy in China were taken from those of geomancy. These two sciences, together with astrology, were originally united in a system that recognized correspondences between planetary influences and the spirits of the earth's metals. Here the seven planetary deities represent the seven 'terrestrial planets' in the earth: Jupiter (tin), Mars (iron), Saturn (lead), Mercury (quicksilver), Luna (silver), Sol (gold), and Venus (copper). (The Seven Metals, from J. D. Mylius, *Philosophia Reformata,* 1622.)

THE SEVEN METALS

Here are portrayed
The hidden treasures of the earth;
    And how the stars of the heavens
    Are locked up deep in the mountains.

The earth contains
Its own planets,
    To which the elements
    Give their qualities and powers.

If you doubt who they are
You must look closely
    At all metals.
    Heaven will help you to understand.

8 The active forces in nature proceed from one source but are apparent as two opposites, represented in Eastern metaphysics as the dragon of heaven and the tiger of earth. All the phenomena in creation reflect the varying states of relationship between these two. (Dragon and Tiger, woodcut by Isoda Koryusai, Japan, 18th c.)

9 The bard, prophet and mystic fre-
quent the wild places of the earth,
where the disturbed energies of the
earth spirit disorder the mind and
stimulate the poetic imagination. (The
Bard, painting by Thomas Jones, 1774.)

10, 11 To the native Australians every least feature of the landscape marks the scene of an episode in the histories of the wandering gods by whom the country was formed. These episodes in turn relate to the spiritual potentialities of the spot and are imitated in the rituals performed there. Thus the cycles of animal fertility and plant growth are perpetuated. The significance of this cleft in the rock (below) is conveyed to the initiate by the painted symbols representing the creative forces of nature that are here active. Similar marks to those made by the Australian nomads, and no doubt with an equally precise though now forgotten meaning, were carved on notable rocks and outcrops by the Stone Age tribes of Britain (above). (10 Incised rock at Routing Lynn, from *Incised Markings on Stone, Northumberland,* 1869; 11 Cave painting, North Kimberleys, Western Australia.)

12 Demeter, the goddess of the earth's fertility, was naturally revered by the early agriculturists. Her daughter Persephone was abducted by Pluto the ruler of Tartaros the abyss, and Demeter wandered the earth in search of her. Having learnt of her fate, Demeter desolated the earth until Persephone was restored to her for an annual period. So were instituted the seasons of the agricultural year. In return for the kindness shown to her in her wanderings by the people of Eleusis, Demeter revealed to them the mysteries of her function, and these were imparted to initiates in rituals that included dramatic performances of Demeter's legend. Here she appears with her attributes, the sickle and the sheaf of corn, and her attendant bears the double-headed axe, symbol of the mysteries. (Watercolour by Thomas Stothard, early 19th c.)

13 Spirit accumulates in underground caverns, and such places are universally recognized as appropriate for the invocation and direction of the forces of nature. This cavern near Chichén Itzá is used for rituals to stimulate the spirits that bring rain. (Cave with Maya offerings at Balancanché, Yucatán, Mexico.)

14 The virgin spirit of the earth, personified by St Geneviève, patron saint of
Paris, presides over a miniature golden age within the sacred fane of a megalithic
temple. The location of the stone circle is unknown, as is the episode in the legend
of the saint here illustrated, but the occult symbol of the virgin within the temenos
or sacred enclosure refers to the ancient practice of siting temples at centres of
terrestrial energy, over buried springs or fissures, where resides the spirit that is
invoked by priest or mystic. (St Geneviève with her Flock, painting, France,
late 16th c.)

15 In the Celtic parts of western Europe certain boulders and ancient erected stones have retained into the present time a reputation as centres of spiritual activity and are resorted to by childless women for their fertilizing properties. It is recognized in traditionalist societies throughout the world that such rocks are receptacles of the vital spirit that animates nature. (Menhir, Brittany.)

16 In the ancient theology a cave was the symbol of the whole world and was considered to provide a passage for the dead descending into Tartaros and for the ascent of gods and souls coming into generation. William Blake's view of the world and the flow of spirit that animates it was inspired by Porphyry's *Cave of the Nymphs,* which is a profound and mystical commentary on the cave in the island of Ithaca described by Homer. (The Cycle of the Life of Man, tempera painting by William Blake, England, 1821.)

17 A tree is another symbol of the world, for its roots and branches reach from Tartaros to the heavens and its fruit is the product of the waters and minerals of the earth and the power of the sun. Virgil described the ash as the tree noted for its long life span, whose roots reach as far below as its branches above, and it was the ash tree that the Scandinavians took to represent Yggdrasill, the universal system, as described in the Eddas, in which the earth in the centre is encircled by the Midgard serpent, its vital principle. (Yggdrasill, the Mundane Tree, frontispiece of *Northern Antiquities* by Bishop Percy, 1847.)

FONTIS NYMPHA SACRI SOMNV
NE RVMPE QVIESCO ·

18 The natural perception of the Irish country people preserves their contacts with the spirits of the land. At a crossroads by a stream a thorn bush grows over the base of a stone cross, where, the shaft having been removed, water gathers in a shallow stoop. If the right procedure is followed and a rag offering left on a branch of the thorn, this water, or the spirit that resides in it, will cure people of warts without the intercession of priest or doctor. (Roadside well, Co. Leix, Ireland.)

19 A secluded spot where waters trickle from a grotto is inherently attractive to the spirits of men and nature. The palpable sanctity of such a place, a natural altar for invoking the subtle powers of the earth, is here impersonated by the nymph of the holy fountain. (The Nymph of the Spring, painting by Lucas Cranach, Germany, c. 1518.)

20, 21 By universal account, spirit is attracted to colour and gaiety and may be
influenced to assume its most benevolent aspect by ritual correctly performed.
Prayer flags at a Buddhist shrine in Bhutan enliven the spirits of the country
and its inhabitants. The native Shinto religion of Japan recognizes the spirits
of the country and locates them in shrines, each one designed to suit the requirements of the resident spirit. Here, as in all other parts of the world, a
thorn tree hung with strips of paper or cloth is noted as an attraction to spirit,
encouraging in it a favourable attitude to the welfare of the people. (20 Gohei
or 'paper prayers' at Heian shrine, Kyoto, Japan; 21 Mani shrine of Dju
Gömpa, Bhutan.)

22 The flow of earth current is affected by underground streams and veins of ore, and over these its intensified activity is apparent to those who can divine it. As here illustrated, mines may be located by the dowser's rod. An earlier use for the dowser's sensitivity was in geomancy. A temple or shrine is obviously useless without a spirit to inhabit it, so its correct location relative to the natural paths and centres of the earth spirit was the first consideration of the ancient architects. (Tracing mineral lodes with a diviner's rod, from Roessler, *Speculum metallurgicum politissimum*, 1700.)

23 The geomancer having found the site for a temple, the architect stretches a line from the foundation pole towards the heavenly body that corresponds to the tutelary god of the place. The Roman augur, if only in form, continued the antique practice, and it was from that classical tradition that Hogarth derived his allegorical view of a temple's foundation. (Frontispiece by William Hogarth for Kirby, *Perspective of Architecture*, England, 1760.)

24 The sparkling fountains of the Seven Springs at Bisley, Gloucestershire, have never failed even in times of long drought. For this the people dress them with flowers on Ascension Day. The screen through which they pour was restored in 1868 and bears the inscription:

O YE WELLS BLESS YE THE LORD:
PRAISE HIM AND MAGNIFY HIM FOR EVER.

25 Stagnant water will satisfy thirst, but the fresh clear water of a spring also heals body and soul by virtue of the spirit that is in it. In gratitude for these benefits, and to ensure their continuation, it is an old custom to decorate a spring at its proper season with flowers or other offerings. This custom is most actively observed in Derbyshire, where every summer the springs and wells are dressed with flower petals, each village having its traditional methods and motifs. (Decorated well at Tissington, Derbyshire, England.)

DAVID AND GOLIATH

26 Placed high above the clouds in a Chinese mountain landscape by the laws of feng-shui, this pavilion affords a view of the world as seen by the gods. It is dedicated to the game of chess: a fine place for a Masters' tournament. (Chess pavilion on one of the peaks of the Hua-shan, Shangsi, China.)

27 One of the most powerful and dramatic of the native sanctuaries in Germany is the Externsteine rocks. The place has influenced every stage in the country's history. It was a ritual centre for the old tribes of reindeer hunters, later a place of assembly, judgment and initiation, a refuge of Christian anchorites and the scene of spirit-generating Nazi ceremonies under the direction of Himmler. Now it receives family tourist parties as a neutral 'place of nature and culture'. All that is characteristic of a religious centre is present at the rocks. Near the summit of the tallest spire is a carved-out chapel orientated to receive the light of midwinter sunrise; below is a crypt and well. The ancient significance of the place is disputed with great bitterness by rival archaeologists, but its attraction for mystics is eternal and obvious. (Externsteine, near Horn, Lippe, lithograph by E. Zeiss, Germany, c. 1860.)

28 The legends of Cornwall and Somerset insist that Jesus came to England with St Joseph of Arimathaea, who was engaged in the tin trade. On Weary-all Hill above Glastonbury, St Joseph planted his staff which grew into the famous thorn tree that blossomed every year on the anniversary of Christ's birth. The site of the original tree, hacked down at the Reformation, is marked by a stone, but its descendants continue to flower at the proper time, and the Monarch by tradition receives a sprig on Christmas Day. (The Holy Thorn in blossom, Glastonbury, Somerset, England.)

29 The traditional birthplace of Jesus at Bethlehem is not a stable but a grotto, and so, like Dionysus, Hermes, Apollo and many other gods, he was born from the womb of the earth, the offspring of the virgin spirit. (The Adoration of the Shepherds, by Giorgione, c. 1478–1510.)

30 Killing the dragon is a feat attributed to many gods, saints and heroes, and it occurs as a symbol in the language of alchemy, from which the Christian symbol of St Michael and the dragon was developed. In such a context it signifies the purification of the earth spirit, and the removal of its serpent venom by means of a pole or pillar planted in the ground and serving as an instrument for the union of cosmic and terrestrial forces. (St Michael, engraving by Martin Schongauer, Germany, c. 1450–1491.)

31 From the head of the White Horse, carved at some remote but unknown date in the chalk of the Berkshire Downs (now confusingly transferred to Oxfordshire), Dragon Hill is visible in the middle distance. The patch of bare chalk on its crown marks the place where St George killed the dragon, whose poisonous blood has ever since made it impossible for grass to grow there. (Dragon Hill, Uffington, Oxfordshire, England.)

32 When Brute the Trojan, t
first of the British kings accor
ing to the old histories, landed
Devon, he found the count
populated by giants, a race that
still remembered in West Cou
try legend as having built t
ancient stone monuments a
shaped the natural features of t
landscape. The memory of t
old giants was preserved at fea
and fairs down to the time of t
Reformation, when such popu
manifestations of true poetic a
religious instinct were suppress
in the interests of rationalism a
morality. This twelve-foot-hi
wicker giant, last seen mould
ing away in the old Tailors' Ha
Salisbury, towards the middle
the nineteenth century, was call
St Christopher and used to para
the streets at the annual fair in t
company of suitably grotesc
attendants. He was the last of t
perambulating giants of Englan

33 St Christopher the Chr
bearer has long been a favour
among the saints of the Calend
from which the Pope has recen
excluded him; for in his pers
the old giants of the earth retur
to infiltrate the Church. His la
and sometimes monstrous fra
– in the Greek Church he
depicted with a dog's or wo
head like Anubis – is often pain
on church walls. (St Christoph
painting by Quentin Mas
Flanders, c. 1490.)

34–36 St Michael, the archangel who leads the heavenly hosts, reigns over the high places, and hilltop churches are often dedicated to him in succession to the corresponding god of the old astronomical religion. Typical altars of St Michael are on the ancient sanctuary, the Needle Rock, at Le Puy in France, Burrowbridge Hill in the Somerset marshes, and the famous Tor at Glastonbury. (34 Rocher d'Aiguille, Le Puy, Haute-Loire, France; 35 Glastonbury Tor with St Michael's Church, Somerset, England; 36 Burrowbridge Hill, Somerset, England.

37 In metaphysical language a mountain represents the state of vision; in terms of dynamics it is a generator of the energy that inspires the high state of madness or prophecy; and so, following the law of correspondences, it provides an appropriate rostrum for prophets and preachers. Rocks were revered by the ancients for their oracular properties, and the tradition is here observed by Claude, who depicts the Sermon on the Mount on a rocky knoll, the sort of place where John Wesley often chose to address his followers. (The Sermon on the Mount, painting by Claude Lorrain, France, 1656.)

38 The plan of Firuzabad is the image of the spherical universe of ancient cosmology. In the centre is the citadel rock, the dynamic centre, representing the axis of the universe, the canon of eternal law and the true self in human nature. The city only dies when the citadel surrenders. (Firuzabad or Fars, Iran, 3rd century AD.)

39 The power of the spirit that pervades the great rocks is drawn out to the benefit of all living things by the ceremonies of the native Australians. By their intimate knowledge of the local spirit world (and consequently of its product, physical nature) they are able to live without material encumbrance in country that otherwise would be desert. (Corroboree Rock, central Australia.)

40 The cosmological centre of the Islamic world is marked by the black meteorite, the Kaaba stone at Mecca, towards which Moslems turn in their daily prayers. (Muhammad and the Black Stone, from Rashid-al-Din's *Universal History*, A D 1307–8.)

41 The Rock of Foundation at Jerusalem is for the Jews the centre of the world, and every other nation once had its own cosmological centre, where the harmony of the universe was imitated in architecture and ritual. In opposition to the former cosmic religion and the spherical universe of the ancient astronomers, Cosmas, a sixth-century Christian geographer, declared the earth to be flat and in the centre of the universe and Jerusalem to be at the centre of the earth. This cosmology became an idol to the medieval Church and to dispute its literal truth a heresy. So the profound and subtle allegories of the ancient philosophers were transformed into repressive dogma. (Map of the World with Jerusalem at the centre, English psalter, 13th c.; see p. 79.)

42 A palace retains the solar power of the emperor and, like all centres of government throughout the world, is approached by long straight avenues which conduct the power throughout the kingdom and at the same time draw into the centre the tribute of the countryside and people. Versailles, the seat of the Sun King, was laid out to function as a solar centre by Le Nôtre in the 17th century. (The Château de Versailles, detail of painting by Pierre Patel, France, *c.* 1668.)

43 The power of the eighteenth-century English landowner over his surroundings was symbolized by the avenues radiating from his solar residence. Architects followed the geomantic tradition of laying avenues to distant spires and landscape features. When the country aristocracy lost its economic and political supremacy, the avenues were no longer appropriate and were broken up, and the big houses, deprived of local sustenance and of their function as power-dispensers, went into decline. This photograph shows Cirencester Church on the line of the Broad Ride, one of several straight tracks that are aligned on its ancient site. These include stretches of prehistoric track, some with Roman paving, on Akeman Street, Ermin Way and Foss Way. (The Broad Ride, Cirencester Park, Gloucestershire, England.)

44 Towering above the sacred landscape of the Teutoburger Wald, where the heroic German myths are localized, is the giant image of Arminius or Hermann, the warrior who defeated the Roman legions. The monument was erected as a symbol of national unity and a generator of national spirit. It is approached by a processional way past the shrines of other heroes, and may be contemplated from a courtyard as at the royal tombs of China. (Hermannsdenkmal, by E. von Bandel, Lippe, Germany, 1875.)

45 The story of Babel in Genesis 11 describes the end of the cycle of civilization that begins with settlement, agriculture and building and ends with the downfall of the monstrous structure that men have imposed on nature. Like Plato's Atlantis it illustrates the traditional belief that such cycles have occurred in the remote past, and explains why the ancients cultivated the art of geomancy, the use of proportion in architecture and the canonical harmonies in music as means of ordering human society in accordance with natural law and preventing the development of Babel or Babylon. (The Building of the Tower of Babel, painting by Pieter Bruegel the Elder, Flanders, 16th c.)

46 The nineteenth-century landscape sacred and desecrated. The reverend poet George Herbert portrayed by William Dyce, a master at illustrating the numinous in landscape. In the background the soaring spire of Salisbury Cathedral, visible for miles across the flat meadows of the Avon valley, sanctifies its surroundings and provides a positive yang element to balance the yin scenery of its setting. (George Herbert at Bemerton, painting by William Dyce, England, 1861.)

47 'The completely profane world, the wholly
desacralized cosmos, is a recent discovery in the
history of the human spirit.' (Mircea Eliade,
The Sacred and the Profane.) The tall chimneys
of industrialized landscape symbolize the exces-
sive dominance of the masculine yang force and
its values. The spirits of nature are expelled
from their haunts in tree, hill and stream, and
the country is left sterile and dead, a monument
to the consequences of human rapacity un-
checked by considerations of spirit. (Landscape
in the Borinage, painting by Constantin
Meunier, Belgium, late 19th c.)

48 Total archaeology in progress. The destruction of this Mississippi mound in 1850, fortunately recorded by a meticulous artist, provided evidence of the cosmically ordered society of the ancient American Indians. Seasonal assemblies at such places were conducted in imitation of the heavenly hierarchy. (Dr Dickenson excavating a mound, detail of the Mississippi Panorama by John Egan, USA, 1850.)

Engraved by W Blake 1773 from an old Italian Drawing
This is One of the Gothic Artists who Built the Cathedrals in what we call the Dark Ages
Wandering about in sheep skins & goat skins of whom the World was not worthy
Michael Angelo Pinxit   such were the Christians
                                  in all Ages

Documentary illustrations and commentaries

Albion

'All things begin and end on Albion's ancient, Druid, rocky shore', wrote William Blake, which explains why this book is somewhat nationally orientated. The great themes of mythology are the property of every race, and the recognition of spirit is not confined to particular countries or cultures. It is active everywhere, and illustrations drawn from one part of the world are relevant to any other. Forms and customs vary locally, but their reference to the reality of the spirit world is at all times the same. Unity of experience was at the foundation of the ancient universal religion. It is an old belief that St Joseph of Arimathaea with his nephew, Jesus, visited England, and it is perfectly in accordance with poetic truth that Blake should picture him as both the native genius of Britain and a Gothic mason.

1 Joseph of Arimathaea among the rocks of Albion, engraving by William Blake, England, 1773. (British Museum, London.)

HOWE L SELE'S OAK

2

THE SALCEY OAK

3

THE OLD OAK

MALCOLM
LODWICK

4

Receptacles of the earth spirit: trees

All shrines and temples are in a way symbols of the entire creation, and trees are peculiarly adapted to this character for the reasons set out in the text to pl. 17. They are regarded as residences of spirit, particularly when they are isolated or remarkable in form, or where they grow on a spot of traditional sanctity. It is an old custom, still remembered in parts of Britain, to replace a sacred tree in decay with a sapling of the same species.

A person today who holds conversation with trees is liable to find himself under medical supervision far removed from sylvan influence. In the ancient world however, and throughout the greater part of history, trees were considered the most respectable and enlightening companions, and it was the custom to ask their advice on the highest matters of state. They directed the wanderings of the earliest tribes, nor did civilization remove their influence. The Greeks consulted Apollo's laurel at Delphi and the oak of Zeus at Dodona, the Druid priests were intimate with the oracular oak, and the warning voice of the grove of Vesta saved Rome from attack by the Gauls. The Church and human pride destroyed the old relationship between men and trees, and so Joan of Arc, inspired by a tree spirit, was burnt for observing the orthodox prophetic tradition.

2 A metal plaque marks the spot by the Dolgellau to Llanfachreth road in Merioneth where stood the ominous 'hollow tree of the spirit' which fell in 1813. It had long been known as a haunt of spirits, and in 1402 its hollow trunk concealed the corpse of the local chieftain, Hywel Selau, murdered by Owain Glyndwr. The tree had already been struck by lightning, and now it became the residence of the ghost of the murdered man. On this account it was locally dreaded and shunned after dark. (Mary Roberts, *Ruins and Old Trees, c.* 1880.)

3 Another old sacred tree, the Salcey Oak, forty feet in girth, illustrates the romantic appeal of rotting timber. (Mary Roberts, *Ruins and Old Trees, c.* 1880.)

4 Behind some broken railings in the middle of a busy crossroads in Carmarthen town stands a rough concrete pillar from which protrude a few blackened sticks – all that remains of Merlin's sacred oak. A most curious monument. Plans to demolish it or move it to the side of the road are defeated by the memory of Merlin's prophecy that when the oak no longer stands, Carmarthen too will fall. And so it may, for the same interests that would remove the oak also favour pulling down the town for redevelopment. (Drawing by Malcolm Lodwick.)

5 Artist's view of the prophetic oak in the precincts of the Temple of Zeus at Dodona, as it was *c.* 200 BC. (*Temples and Sanctuaries of Ancient Greece*, London and New York 1971.)

6 The sacred Chapel Oak of Allouville, Normandy, accommodates its spirits in an artificial shrine. (Drawing by Marquis, 1824.)

7 The Major Oak of Sherwood Forest, Nottinghamshire, the last and greatest of the old forest oaks, 64 feet round and capable of holding 34 children within its trunk. This is an example of the autonomous development of a tree into a popular shrine, for it is much sought out by tourists, and on August Bank Holiday 1957 it was estimated that 15,000 people came to see it.

5

6

7

Receptacles of the earth spirit: springs, wells and rivers

Where fresh water runs there runs spirit, and this is particularly so wherever water springs up from below the earth, for it comes from the realm of the earth goddess and bears her gifts. Properly every spring has its season of efficacy when its virtues are most generously displayed. In times before doctors, psychiatrists, marriage guidance officials, newspaper horoscopes, drugs and artificial fertilizers, all their functions were exercised by the spirits of the local springs, who required no payment but respect and attention. Yet it is the custom, wherever use is still found for the spirits in water, to reward their benevolence with gifts of coins, rags and trinkets, for spirit is believed to agree with magpies, jackdaws and children in its taste for glittering objects.

Ancient science had much use for the spirit in water. The holy well in the crypts of many cathedrals and churches is the original pre-Christian shrine. It accommodates the spirit of the place and provides the earth and lunar element (water being under the influence of the moon) to balance the solar invocation of the edifice. A temple, as an image of the universe, must comprehend all in nature, and so all ancient sacred sites have wells, springs, underground streams or catacombs in their foundations. Placed elsewhere than by a natural location of spirit, a temple would lack the medium it was designed to manipulate.

The Celtic Church in Britain was a reformation of Druidism and preached a return to simple reliance on the gifts of the earth spirit at rock, well and fountain. The relics of its baptistries and oratories are still found throughout the Celtic world, particularly dense in Cornwall.

8 Holy well at Roche, thus described last century by J.P. Blight: 'The spring is still in repute, and is frequented by the peasantry, before sunrise, on holy Thursday and the two following Thursdays; the blessing of the tutelary saint is bespoken by the offering of pins, sometimes bent before thrown into the water.' (J.T. Blight, *Ancient Crosses and Other Antiquities of Cornwall*, Penzance 1872.)

9 Blight's drawing of St John's holy well, Morwenstow, with the vicar, the Reverend R.S. Hawker, latter-day Celtic saint, poet and mystic. (J. T. Blight, *Ancient Crosses and Other Antiquities of Cornwall*, Penzance 1872.)

10 The ancient stones of the megalith builders are in many cases located over springs, and appear to have been designed as permanent residences for the fluctuating spirit of the waters. At Calmsden near Cirencester, Gloucestershire, an old stone cross stands over a sacred spring that once gave the village its water supply. (Charles Pooley, *Notes on the Old Crosses of Gloucestershire*, London 1868.)

11 The Cornish well of St Keyne has the remarkable property of giving supremacy in marriage to whichever one of a couple shall first drink of its waters. The woman saint who founded it planted over it four symbolic trees, oak, ash, elm and withy, all four, it was said, growing on one stem. They blew down in a storm in 1703 and were replaced by others. (M. and L. Quiller-Couch, *Ancient Holy Wells of Cornwall*, 1894.)

12 Spirit has infinite local forms but is everywhere of the same nature. There is therefore a detectable unity in the forms created and inhabited by spirit, whether in the roots or branches of a tree or in this aerial view of the Colorado River. (*Die Welt von oben*, Munich 1966.)

11

12

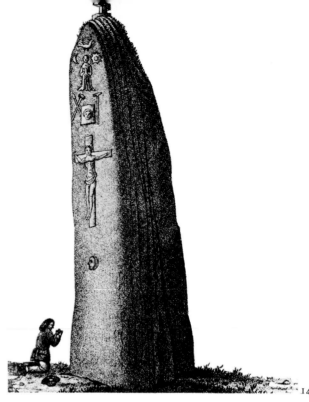

13

14

Receptacles of the earth spirit: rocks and mountains

Everywhere that men have been on earth they have discovered aboriginal inhabitants in the form of spirits from whom they have inherited the secrets of the landscape. A dying or departing race has always passed on to its successors the local mystical knowledge, and it is only in modern times that the tradition has been lost by the appearance, as in North America, of a people who did not care to receive it. Violence, restlessness, drink and crank religions are the compensations of the alienated, and the power of the electric generator substitutes for the lost power of natural invocation.

Power, as every mystic knows, adheres to the rocky places. In rocks were the first temples, natural settings for contact with spirit. Every rock has its proper name according to its cosmogonic meaning and spiritual purpose, and where the names have been lost, practical knowledge has been lost with them.

15

16

13 Catholic priest invoking, exorcizing or reading to the spirit in the sacred rock at the church of Saint-Julien in Le Mans, France. (Engraving by Jorand and Fragonard.)

14 The menhir of Saint-Duzec in Brittany is carved with the emblems of the Crucifixion, the more decently to receive the supplications traditionally addressed to it by the people. (*Guide de la Bretagne*, 19th c.)

15 Rocking stones, poised by nature, art or both so that they can be set moving by the touch of a hand yet never lose their equilibrium, were formerly used as instruments of magic and divination. Leaders and initiates were tested by such a stone, which might refuse to rock if they were unworthy. Oracles were inspired by the sound of the rocking stone and the energy it generated. (Pierre tremblante, Brech, Morbihan, France.)

16 Rocky islands off the coast are favourite residences of spirit and therefore of anchorites and mystics. St Michael's Mount in Cornwall, like its twin island by the opposite coast of Normandy, was the scene of a personal appearance by the Archangel in the Middle Ages. (St Michael's Mount, after H. Gastineau, 19th c.)

17 A rare sacred rock of the Church of England, sanctified by the bardic adventure of the Reverend Toplady of Burrington Combe, Somerset, who, while sheltering from the rain in a crevice of the rock, was inspired to compose the hymn beginning: 'Rock of Ages, cleft for me, let me hide myself in thee.'

18 The cosmological centre of the Jewish and Christian worlds is the rock of Jerusalem, where Noah's flood was sucked down into the earth from which it will one day rise again. (The Dome of the Rock, Jerusalem; see pl. 41.)

17

18

Receptacles of the earth spirit: clefts and caverns

A cavern, according to ancient theology, is a gateway to the lower kingdom, a passage for spirits descending into Tartaros and rising again into generation. Cracks in the earth bring to the surface the influences of the earth goddess. The cleft rock from which issued the vapours that inspired the oracle gave its name to Delphi, meaning 'vagina', and so the cavern has become a favourite repository for the sexual fantasies of Freudians. Its primary reference, however, is to something more profound than human sexuality; for the cave is not only a place of shelter and renewal, but a natural temple of initiation, where the earth goddess, naked and terrifying, reveals her most intimate secrets to those brave enough to penetrate her chamber. The state magicians of Babylon were initiated underground and the practice was common throughout the ancient world. At the oracle of Trophonius near Mount Helicon in Boeotia the experience of the descent and confrontation with the goddess was so dreadful that whoever underwent it was said never to smile again. Yet the Greeks were generally on familiar terms with the spirits of the underworld, and did not fear them in the way people do in times when religion ignores the chthonic element in spiritual nature. Solar religion with its emphasis on the light of reason avoids the irrational world of the cavern and the dark recesses of the mind, and so the realm of the goddess is transformed by ignorance into the abyss of Satan, producing sickness and sterility on earth and diseased imaginations in men.

19

20

21

22

19 Delphi, said to be one of the most naturally impressive places in the world, was the seat of the famous oracle whose knowledge was acquired from the influences of the earth goddess rising from a cleft in the rock. Originally a natural earth oracle operating at only one season in the year, it was taken over by the priests of Apollo, who fixed its energies and made its productions continuous. (The large Temple of Apollo, Delphi, Greece.)

20 Mithras was a rock-born god, whose cult was popular in Rome at the beginning of Christianity, and his mysteries were properly celebrated in underground caverns. His influence was for personal vision and achievement. (Mithraic altar below the Basilica of San Clemente, Rome, 3rd c. AD.)

21 Megalithic dolmens are situated over springs or fissures and serve to concentrate the earth spirit for magical purposes. At Plouaret, Brittany, the present chapel replaces an earlier one built over a megalithic chamber, where Mass is now celebrated on Sundays. (Chapelle des Sept Saints, Plouaret, Côtes-du-Nord, France.)

22 The adventures of gods and local spirits at the natural shrines of the countryside were reinterpreted under Christianity as episodes in the legends of saints. This oracular cavern, a place of vigils and visions, is in the sheer cliff above the Lake at Glendalough, Co. Wicklow, where an old centre of Druid learning was taken over by St Kevin in the sixth century. The cave is now known as St Kevin's Bed.

23 The earth spirit, as the Virgin, sanctifies for Irish Catholics the entrance to the grotto. Deeper inside the earth she is represented by the black Virgin of the crypt, whose cult is unknown to the modern Church. (Sacred grotto at Kilnacanogh, Co. Wicklow, Ireland.)

24 Descent into the underworld is a universal theme in religion, alchemical symbolism and mystical experience. It represents a stage in initiation and precedes the promised achievement of paradise on earth. In the early Christian Gnostic myth Christ penetrated the depths of hell to free the souls of the damned. The simple-minded followed him gladly, but the former priests and bishops there confined, having been so often misled in their lifetimes, refused the offer of release, suspecting it to be yet another trick. The gateway to the underworld, as here illustrated, is the traditional rocky cavern. (The Harrowing of Hell, painting by Giovanni Bellini, Italy, c. 1500, Bristol Art Gallery.)

23 24

ΣΩΤΗΡ
ΚΟΣΜΟΥ

25

26

27 28

Functions of the earth spirit: fertilizing

29

30

An earlier generation of anthropologists used to claim that people of certain traditionalist societies were ignorant of the physical causes of procreation and attributed babies to the intervention of spirits. The misunderstanding arose because the natives, while recognizing the physical processes of birth, recognized also that a child is not simply the issue of its parents' union (were it so, variations would accumulate, and in the course of a few generations the human type would be unrecognizable); but a product of the earth spirit and the astrological influences at its time and place of birth. From the hints of Plato it appears that the determination of the proper dates for conceiving children survived as an occult science in his time, for he recommends it to the citizens of his republic as a method of eugenics. The practice was regulated by the dates and places of festivals, for the endemic fever of sexuality that is now a feature of city life is peculiar to that environment, the ancients being more inclined to follow the example of the animal world, confining their sexual activity to certain times of the year and under the influence of a god.

The fertility rites that invoked the generative spirit and kept up the numbers of the people were also, by the magical principle of correspondences, effective in bringing about the reproduction of animals and plants. So in Australia every species has its own increase centres, where the proper ritual by the natives releases its *karunba*, life essence. Respectable pagan religious festivals featured exhibitions of emblematic male and female organs and the erection of phallic pillars, partly, we are told, to familiarize people with their own natures and partly to increase the fertility of the earth. Tall menhirs and suggestively shaped rocks are often, as repositories of fertilizing spirit, places of resort for childless women, a custom which doubtless perpetuates their ancient function.

25 The male organ erect was the symbol in ancient religion of the generative power in the universe, effective on earth as the fertilizing energy of the sun. The gnostics, who reconciled the new Christian religion with the philosophy of the old, displayed to their initiates such images as these, the central figure bearing the inscription SAVIOUR OF THE WORLD. (R.P. Knight and others, *Account of the worship of Priapus . . .*, London 1786.)

26 The fertilizing energy animating this Brittany menhir, still on its original site at Kernuz, is signified by the ascending serpent and by the carved gods, the Celtic correspondences of Mercurius and Hercules.

27 Stones sacred to Hermes stood in line by the paths leading to the central places of assembly in ancient Greece, pointing towards the axis stone at the crossroads. Their evident function as symbols and conductors of the mercurial spirit of fertility in the earth can also be attributed to the stone crosses in Celtic lands which have similar characteristics. (Herm, National Archaeological Museum, Athens.)

28, 30 The nature of the ancient science in connection with the fertility of the earth is clearly expressed in the forms of its two types of instruments. The tall stone concentrates the positive forces of the cosmos and penetrates the body of the earth, whose negative, receptive spirit has its characteristic location in the holy well. (28 Menhir, Porspoder, Finistère, France; 30 Holy well in the West of Ireland.)

29 At Locronon in Brittany is the 'Stone Mare', said to have been a sacred Druid rock, whose spirit is invoked by childless women. (Ar Gazeck Van, Locronon, Finistère, France.)

30 See 28.

31

Functions of the earth spirit: therapeutic

Conventions of geomancy place every country, district and piece of land under the influence of a particular astrological sign, whose attributes are reflected in local character. Correspondences between these symbols and the parts of the body reveal themselves in the therapeutic powers of the earth spirit at local wells and places of healing. One such place may be known for its virtue in cases of rheumatism, another benefits the eyes, each according to its astrological type. Chemists may find no particular qualities in the waters of a healing well to account for its efficacy; but the water is a symbol; the power of healing comes from spirit. That is why the therapeutic shrines of the earth spirit are approached in a ritualistic manner, why rag or token offerings are left there and a certain procedure is followed that the local spirits find seemly. A Dublin businessman recently observed in conversation that to obtain proper results from a visit to a holy well it is necessary to leave one's car behind.

35

32

33

34

BLADUD,
To whom the GRECIANS gave the Name of
ABARIS.

31 The holy well at St Breward was famous for curing sore eyes. (M. & L. Quiller-Couch, *Ancient and Holy Wells of Cornwall*, 1894.)

32 This dim snapshot by the author of *The Ancient Springs, Wells and Holy Wells of Gloucestershire* shows a lame boy attending the healing Hemlock Well, 'a miniature Lourdes in the middle of Stroud'. (R. C. S. Walters, *The Ancient Springs . . .*, Bristol 1928.)

33 The unique megalithic relic called Men-an-tol on the west Cornish moors is locally known as an instrument of divination and healing. It was the practice to pass scrofulous children through the holed stone and draw them three times round on the grass against the sun. All sorts of pains were found to be cured by such means, and sporting or pious tourists are still often to be seen squeezing through the ring. (J. T. Blight, *A Week at the Land's End*, London 1861.)

34 The healing spring of the Virgin at Josselin in Brittany is the object of a yearly pilgrimage intended to avert the curse laid on the people by the Virgin herself, who was driven away by the women at the spring of whom she asked a drink of water. In consequence they and their descendants were condemned to howl like dogs every Pentecost. The spring is credited with many cures of epilepsy. (Fontaine Notre-Dame, Josselin, Morbihan, France.)

35 The hot springs at Bath are famous for their cures of rheumatism and skin disease, but their virtues are generally disregarded by local doctors who prefer to prescribe drugs from the chemist. The waters were made much of by the Romans, whose temple of Minerva replaced a Celtic establishment founded by Bladud, the Pythagorean necromancer, early aeronaut and ninth king of Britain. This portrait is by John Wood, the mystical Bath architect. (H. Levis, *Bladud of Bath*, repr. West Country Edns, Bath 1973.)

36 A cavern with a sacred spring in the Acropolis at Athens was a shrine of Asclepius, god of healing. His petitioners threw offerings into a pit nearby. (Cave shrine, Acropolis, Athens.)

36

Functions of the earth spirit: oracular

The inspired leader, the prophet and law-giver, draws his powers from above, and his symbolic environment is the high mountain of authority and vision. His yin opposite, the earth oracle, frequents the low watery places, the nooks, crevasses and caverns where the earth spirit is most responsive to the necromancer's invocation. The nature of this spirit is receptive or feminine, so women are the customary attendants at holy wells and prophetic shrines, and there they were formerly sought out by whoever was simple enough to find witlessness or senility in the prophetess no impediment to the utterance of true prophecy. This aspect of the earth spirit communicates with the depths of the mind when its self-conscious activity is stilled, as in sleep, trance or rapture. The power of Delphi is said to have been discovered by a shepherd boy, who happened to rest by the cleft in the rock on the day when it was most active, and fell into a prophetic trance. Civilization and the reliance of government on the oracle's counsels demanded that it be made to function throughout the year. Apollonian religion and the solar technology of ancient science made this possible, but continuous production of oracles could only be achieved by ever more artificial contrivances. These included animal sacrifices for the release of spirit, cold water showers to bring on shivering, and drugs such as the laurel leaves chewed at Delphi. Plutarch has a terrifying story of the prophetess suddenly going mad before a party of foreign visitors whom the priests had been trying to gratify by stimulating the woman to prophetic frenzy.

The decline of Greek oracles took place at the beginning of the Christian era, and the same process has been noticed by the natives in many other countries since. Spirit is a subtle essence and its ways must be constantly studied if they are to remain known. Reliance on institutions and old formal invocations leads ultimately to loss of contact with spirit and the extinction of oracles.

37, 38 Mother Shipton and her oracular cave. The famous sibyl of Knaresborough in Yorkshire was born Ursula Sontheil in July 1488, the daughter of a local witch and her spirit consort. She became widely respected for her prophecies on matters great and small, and all have come true except those not yet tested by history, such as:

The World then to an end shall come
In Nineteen Hundred and Ninety-One.

Mrs Shipton prophesied the introduction of the potato, the invention of automatic locomotion, the aeroplane and the telegraph and many episodes in national and local history. Her gifts were so natural and so artlessly used that she was consulted even by church dignitaries. She died aged 73 at the very hour she had long before predicted. The portrait of the sibyl in front of a crone-shaped rock is from an old inn sign near her well, whose waters turn to stone objects exposed to them. (37 Mother Shipton's Cave, Knaresborough, Yorkshire, England; 38 *The Life and Prophecies of . . . Mother Shipton*, Leeds 1916.)

37

Near this Petrifying Well
I first drew breath as records Tell
MOTHER
SHIPTON.

39 Prophetic rock functioning in Ireland. (Near Killarney, Co. Kerry.)

40 By the church of St Gulval in West Cornwall there was a holy well which, besides curing various ills, was locally used for divining fate and future. At the beginning of the eighteenth century it still had its resident priestess, an old woman living in a cottage nearby, who gave oracles to visitors and revealed under the inspiration of the waters the whereabouts of lost or stolen objects. She may have been the last of her profession in England. Of her well no trace now remains. (J. T. Blight, *A Week at the Land's End*, London 1861.)

41 Two youths visit the fountain of fortune on white horses. One sleeps by the cleft in the earth that inspires prophetic dreams; the other reads the alchemical inscription with its mystical clues to initiation. (Miniature from the *Livre du Cuer d'Amours espris,* by the René Master, France, 15th c., Osterreichische Nationalbibliothek, Vienna.)

42 Augurs, the Roman geomancers, inspecting a flight of birds. By hints gained from close observation of nature the augur read the patterns of the subtle currents of earth and air and inferred the likely development of events. Other duties included the siting and orientation of temples. (Augurs, painting by Salvator Rosa, Italy, 17th c.)

40

41

42

39

The old hidden tracks that lead from one stone cross to another across the wastes of Dartmoor were, according to legend recorded by the poet Hawker, first made by the feet of angels and then used, by way of successive descent into matter, by saint, pilgrim and pedlar. So in all countries there may be discovered a network of mystical routes, sometimes used at festivals only or in connection with ceremonies, for ritual journeys, as funeral routes or corpse paths. A memory of them is contained in the ubiquitous legend of underground tunnels linking ancient sites. Even when their human functions have lapsed, their reputation remains as spirit paths, as haunts of fairies, ghosts or elementals, to be avoided on particular days of the year. Behind this curious relic of spirit consciousness, as it survives in Europe, is a once indigenous code of geomancy, similar to that of China, where veins of spirit in the earth's crust determine the siting of all tombs and buildings, which must not obstruct their flow. In countries where there is still an active tradition of mystical topography, sacred routes, said to be the paths of the spirits who shaped the landscape, go between the ceremonial centres and are followed by initiates in the course of magical journeys. Under the solar religions of civilization and empire, straight paths, laid out by astronomical considerations, unite cosmic and terrestrial influences and signify the development of a technological form of geomancy, in connection with hierarchical society and centralized power. So in times of social upheaval and of consequent spirituality, prophets always urge the people to abandon the broad highway and seek out again the old paths, where 'thou shalt find rest for thy soul'.

43

44

43 Mysterious little gaps, capped with lintels, in old stone walls on Dartmoor and elsewhere were found by the dowser, Mr Guy Underwood, to mark the passage of lines of terrestrial current or 'spirit paths', which can be detected by the dowser's rod. (Guy Underwood, *The Pattern of the Past*, London 1969.)

44 A large black dog, a widely reported type of spirit phenomenon, is occasionally seen to run down this church path at Bishops Cannings in Wiltshire and across the road to where there is a suggestive gap in the hedge.

45 Paddy Baine unwittingly built his house with one corner on a spirit or fairy path. That part of the house was always disturbed and a local geomancer, an old woman, was called in. She advised removing the obtrusive corner, which, as can be seen, was done. The house was then peaceful and so it still remains. (Dermot MacManus, *The Middle Kingdom*, Gerrards Cross 1972.)

46 The old straight tracks of prehistoric Britain, corresponding to the Chinese spirit paths, have generally been obscured by later development. However, the continuity of ancient sacred places on their course, which were generally used as the sites of Christian churches, helped to preserve their alignments, and many of these were rediscovered some fifty years ago by the Hereford archaeologist Alfred Watkins who called them 'leys'. Watkin's photograph of Broad Street in Bristol shows its line passing right through the tower of St John's Church towards St Michael's visible in the distance. Two other Bristol churches stand on the same alignment. (Alfred Watkins, *The Old Straight Track*, London 1925, repr. London 1972.)

47 The Valley of the Thirteen Tombs, near Peking.

45

46

47

Peopling the landscape

It is a peculiar fact, illustrating the correspondence between the worlds of men and spirit, that a country well endowed with spirit attracts a large and lively human population; and conversely, when spirit declines the people do likewise. Throughout this book we examine various aspects of the spirit in the land as it affects the inhabitants, and it will be noticed that the reason in all cases why people choose to recognize the existence of spirit is the practical advantages thence derived. All traditionalist people, primitives as they are misleadingly called, are utterly dependent in their daily lives on knowledge of the ways and seasons of spirit, and the rulers of all ancient states considered the interests of spirit to be identical with the interests of the people. The sciences of antiquity were directly aimed at raising the level of spirit in the country and keeping human institutions in harmony with it. Thus by their knowledge of geomancy the Chinese were able to preserve and emphasize the spiritual qualities of a landscape, which at the same time supported a dense, prosperous population.

The aims of modern science are otherwise. For many years the primacy of spirit, indeed its very existence, has been ignored by the industrialized nations, and the consequences are now fully apparent. Before the rise of Puritanism in England the towns were small but the countryside was populous; life was eventful and the country was as fair and productive as it has never again been since; most people had some land of their own and a share in the common stock and so were personally and locally independent; and there was time for many feasts, fairs and holidays in the course of the year. These were largely suppressed at and after the Reformation together with the rustic games and rituals that stimulated the spirits of men and nature.

Wherever indigenous culture, which means ultimately knowledge of local spirit, has disappeared, depopulation has followed. People do not mind being poor but they do mind being dispirited. The history of rural decline that followed from the enclosures of common lands in England is well known, and so are the events that led to the depopulation of Scotland and the starvation of Ireland, but the prime cause of these disasters has never been properly recognized. For the process is still continuing in Britain and now all over the world. Everywhere people are drawn from the country to be consumed by urban industrialists, and the reason is that everywhere local culture and independence are under attack, and when they succomb, consciousness of the native spirit goes with them. Without this consciousness life becomes at worst physically unsupportable, at best boring, provincial and second-rate. The cause of rural depopulation is not primarily economic but lies in the fact that if the spirit is destroyed the body disintegrates. It is the relationship between men and spirit that determines whether or not a country is habitable; on which account Plato advised the settlers of his proposed ideal republic that, having chosen their territory, they should first of all discover the local shrines of its spirits and institute festivals there on the appropriate days.

48

49

90

It is an old belief, acknowledged by Vitruvius and Proclus and again in our time by Jung, that the forces of nature that shape the different types of landscape on the earth, giving each its peculiar character, tend similarly to shape the features and characters of its inhabitants. Chinese geomancers see a connection between the fates and destinies of the people and the symbolic forms in surrounding nature. Imaginatively shaped and anthropomorphic rocks are everywhere objects of curiosity; to detect their resemblances is a step towards spirit consciousness. They were formerly pointed out to illustrate episodes in mythology and local legend.

50

48 Features of spirit in a sacred tree in India. (Francis Huxley, *The Way of the Sacred*, London 1974.)

49 A sport of nature to encourage speculation about the unifying tendencies of the creative forces or about the Creator's sense of humour.

50 The forms assumed by spirit depend on the quality of human imagination. The two little girls who photographed these fairies in 1917 saw them according to the notions of their time. Here is an illustrated demonstration of the varying effects of vulgar or refined imagination, emphasizing the necessity of exposing children to the influences of harmonious proportion; for the world accepts the imprint of the mind that perceives it. (Edward L. Gardner, *Fairies*, London 1945.)

51 Stone giant's head, known to Victorian tourists as Dr Syntax, near the Land's End, a memory of the aboriginal giants of Cornwall.

52 The head of the Sphynx rock over Wastwater in the Lake District.

51

52

The earth spirit in ancient science

The megalithic monuments and temples of prehistoric Europe are a sore puzzle to archaeologists, because the mathematical accuracy of their construction and the combination of astronomical and topographical considerations behind their siting reveal their builders as belonging to a civilization far more scientifically developed than modern theories of historical progress allow. The science of the megalith builders was evidently of the magical variety, as practised by the Chaldeans and studied by Pythagoras and the occult schools of Greece, a science whose aims and methods are still displayed in the native systems of geomancy in China, the East and Africa.

It is impossible to comprehend ancient in terms of modern science, for the latter is still philosophically disposed to assume the primacy of matter, even though that notion is contradicted by the modern rediscovery of energy or spirit as the formative cause behind the world of appearances. Ancient science developed from a cosmology that recognized the supreme influence of spirit in the creation of forms and in the fortunes of men. It was therefore very different from science as now defined, for it was concerned with spiritual causes and its purpose was to increase the bounty of the earth by stimulating its spirit. Its methods may be inferred from surviving traditions of alchemy, ritual magic and the other departments of occult science which were formerly unified in the high service of geomancy. Its effect, or the effect intended, was to create a golden age on earth.

54

53

53 The temple of Amon-Ra in Egypt, which Sir J. Norman Lockyer found to have been orientated in such a way that at the date of its foundation the last ray of the midsummer sunset would pass down its long axis and penetrate the inner sanctuary.

54 Boscawen-un stone circle near the Land's End in Cornwall. It was one of the three great Gorsedds, conventions of bards and augurs, in Britain. It is also a meeting place of several alignments of standing stones in the surrounding country, which were erected in connection with the megalithic science. (J. T. Blight, *A Week at the Land's End*, London 1861.)

55 Precise alignments of ancient stones near Boscawen-un stone circle. The line bottom left links the circle with four separate menhirs over some three miles. (John Michell, *The Old Stones of Land's End*, London 1974.)

56 The megalithic circle, Ring of Brodgar, on the mainland of Orkney, is in a now lonely district where flourished a populous prehistoric civilization, whose temples and stone instruments are yet preserved. From the centre of this circle two tall menhirs are visible in direct alignment.

57 The great fallen menhir of Locmariaquer near Carnac in Brittany once stood over 60 feet high. How it was transported and set up is unknown, and so is its full purpose, but it has been shown to have acted as a giant marker of extreme positions in the moon's orbit some 4,000 years ago when viewed from other megalithic sites in the neighbourhood. Here its fragments support a team of Breton dancers.

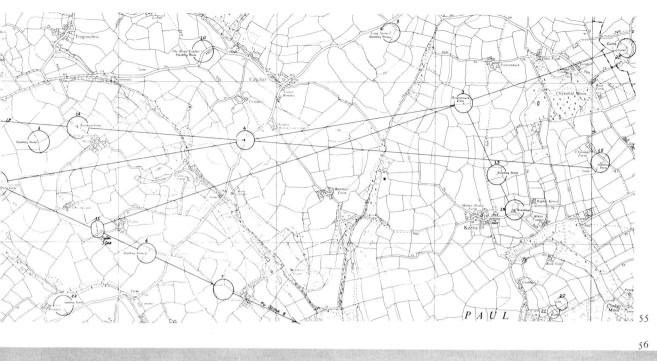

55

56

57

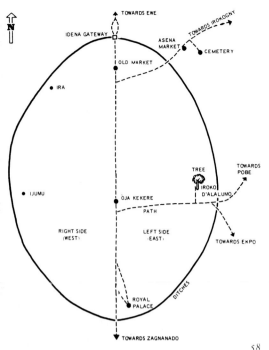

58   59

Settling down

The difficulty with all styles of life, other than the primeval nomadic one, is they involve loss of intimacy with spirit. Settlement breaks the natural flow of communication enjoyed by migrant tribes, and requires the development of artificial means of contact with the ultimate source of life, the spirit of the earth. The life of the natural man is a life of natural ritual, an unconscious reflection of the cosmic order. When it is exchanged for a life of settled civilization, the order must be recreated by contrival ritual. Thus arise the great compensations: religion, philosophy, magic, the arts, crafts and sciences. All these civilized activities are properly intended to investigate the forces active in nature and to direct human energies accordingly; and the first development from a settled relationship between men and earth goddess is geomancy in association with architecture. These arts affect the appearance of the earth, leaving long-lasting traces on the ground; and so the whole earth is marked with patterns of settlement which show, as clearly as any written contract, the terms of the agreement at the time between men and their environment.

58 From camp sites to great cities all settlements are images of their people's cosmological idea. This plan of the Yoruba town of Keta in Dahomey represents a cosmic scheme in which the universal soul is conceived as egg-shaped. The two opposite forces within the universe, yang and yin, corresponding to the east and west halves of the town, revolve about the central axis of eternal law, which in the town is the north-south central line. The only gate is to the north. The siting and significance of every part of the town was determined by the African code of geomancy. (Douglas Fraser, *Village Planning in the Primitive World*. London 1968.)

59 Turner's view of Stonehenge as a condenser of elemental forces. The occult mechanism behind its magnetic attraction is shown in the following diagram. (Stonehenge, drawing by J. M. W. Turner, England 1820–30.)

60 Stonehenge reconstructed in plan with the geometrical scheme superimposed on it that reveals the true nature of this megalithic temple. The scheme here shown is the symbol of the ancient code of cosmology that preserved the stability of past civilizations. Its basic figure is the geometer's allegory, the squared circle, symbol of the ultimate reconciliation within the universe, and within its human microcosm, of all the incommensurable elements, such as body and spirit, that make up the nature of each. The composition of the ancient canon of cosmic law, its symbolic shapes and numbers, its reference to the dimensions of the earth and heavenly bodies and to astrological cycles, its social use and other such things, are set out in the author's *City of Revelation*. The conformity of Stonehenge in all its details to the cosmic canon shows it to be the temple of a society founded on the same principles as the Holy City in St John's Revelation and the ideal community of Plato, all representing the idea of the true, revealed image of universal truth set as the ruling and guiding standard for all people. (John Michell, *City of Revelation*, London 1972.)

61 The extreme consequences of fanatical solar religion are demonstrated in plans for the ceremonial centres of the proposed Thousand-Year Reich. (Märzfeld, project by Albert Speer.)

62 Palma Nuova, the Venetian fortress town, was designed in 1593 according to a geometrical scheme that was intended to dignify military rule and ennoble the minds of the people by the influence of classical proportion. (Palma Nuova, Udine, Italy.)

63 Peking from an aeroplane, the perfect image of an imperial, ceremonial centre, with its long axis, north and south, passing through arches, temples and the sacred hill in the foreground. The power and influence of the round of rituals performed there was transmitted through the agency of the symbolic shape of the city to the whole country. This is geomancy put to the service of centralized government.

60

62

61

63

64

65

Sources of quotations in text

Basilius Valentinus: quoted by C.G. Jung, *Alchemical Studies*, London and New York 1967.

Smohalla: quoted by E.L. Macluhan, *Touch the Earth*, London 1972.

Edward Carpenter, *Civilization: its Cause and Cure*, London 1889.

Mircea Eliade, *The Forge and the Crucible* (English translation), London 1962.

Lord Raglan, *The Temple and the House*, London 1966.

Richard Wilhelm, *I Ching* (English translation by Cary Baynes of Richard Wilhelm's German version), London and New York 1968.

John Michell, *City of Revelation*, London 1972.

A.E. Berriman, *Historical Metrology*, London 1953.

C.H. Hapgood, *Maps of the Ancient Sea Kings*, Philadelphia and New York 1966.

Dermot McManus, *The Middle Kingdom*, Gerrards Cross 1972.

Kathleen Wiltshire, *Ghosts and Legends of the Wiltshire Countryside*, Salisbury 1973.

Winifred Haward, *Hide or Hang*, Clapham (via Lancaster) 1966.

Lascelles Abercrombie, *Town and Country Planning*, London 1947.

Joseph Needham, *Science and Civilization in China*, Cambridge 1954–.

Ernst Börschmann, *Picturesque China*, London 1924.

E.J. Eitel, *Feng-Shui or the Rudiments of Natural Science in China*, London 1873, Cambridge 1973.

Baldwin Spencer and F.J. Gillen, *The Arunta*, London 1927.

Raphael Patai, *Man and Temple*, London 1947.

Mircea Eliade, *The Sacred and the Profane*, New York 1961.

William Cobbett, *History of the Protestant 'Reformation' in England and Ireland*, London 1824.

Objects in the plates reproduced by courtesy of: Allentown, Pa., Art Museum, Samuel H. Kress Collection 33; Arlington Court, National Trust 16; Besançon, Musée Communal 19; Cambridge, Mass., Fogg Museum of Art, Harvard 2; Cardiff, National Museum of Wales 9; Detmold, Lippische Landesbibliothek 27; Edinburgh, University Library 40; London, British Library 7, 41; London, British Museum 6, 8, 23, 30; London, Guildhall Art Gallery 46; London, Science Museum 4; John Michell 12; New York, The Frick Collection 37; Saint-Etienne, Musée de Saint-Etienne 47; St Louis, Mo., St Louis Art Museum 48; Vienna, Kunsthistorisches Museum 45; Washington DC, National Gallery of Art, Samuel H. Kress Collection 29.

Photographs supplied by: Aerofilms Ltd doc. 62; M. Andrain-Arthaud doc. 18; Roloff Beny 20; British Library 7, 41; British Museum 30; Camera Press 11; J. Allan Cash doc. 7; Harold Chapman 24, 35; Courtauld Institute of Art, London doc. 42; Cramers Kunstanstalt, Dortmund 44; William Fix doc. 29, 44; U. and A. Gansser 21; W.E. Garrett 26; G. Gerster-Hillelson 1; Giraudon 14; I. Groth 13; Martin Hürlimann 34; Richard Lannoy doc. 48; Tony Linck 5; Mansell-Alinari doc. 20, 64; Pacific Air Industries doc. 12; Photo Precision Ltd 16, 25; Roger-Viollet 15, doc. 14, 28, 36; Rosmarie Pierer doc. 21; E. Schmidt 38; Edwin Smith 31, 43, doc. 23, 36, 39; Courtesy of the Smithsonian Institution, Freer Gallery of Art, Washington DC doc. 47; Colin Smythe doc. 45; Brian Walker 28.

Landscape symbolism

The eye of the geomancer discerns the symbolic forms in the natural features of a landscape and sees them as influencing the character of the district and its people. In the ancient world such forms were emphasized in the siting and orientation of temples, from which their likenesses were seen most clearly at a certain time of the year when the shadows were right. At such a time the symbol was activated in connection with a cycle of myth and ritual. Here between the stone horns at Knossos, symbol of the active power of the earth goddess, appears Mount Jouctas, 'the horned mountain' or 'the head of Zeus' as it is locally known. The mountain is the mythological residence of Zeus, and at times it looks exactly like a man's head on a dish, a recurrent symbol associated with St John the Baptist and the Celtic hero, Bran.

64 The Horns of Consecration, Palace of Minos, Knossos, Crete.

65 Head of a Martyr, charcoal drawing by Odilon Redon, France 1877. (Rijksmuseum Kröller-Müller, Otterlo.)